Life After Bristol Rovers

SECOND SERIES

The Author

It was in the very early sixties that Mark Leesdad made his first visit to Eastville Stadium, autograph book in hand, to watch the likes of Bradford and Jones, Mabbutt and Davis. Later on, like many teenagers, he exchanged watching for playing and, although there was never any real danger of his becoming the next Harold Jarman (right wing was Mark's favoured position) he did once score for Court Rangers against a Bristol Rovers youth team that he's sure included Frankie Prince.

On the career front Mark learnt his trade as a 'wordsmith' with two major companies, acting as editor of their in-house magazines, handling press enquiries and working with the media. Nowadays he writes sports articles, including his weekly Memory Lane column, for *The Sunday Independent*.

Married to Jan for over thirty years, the couple have two sons, two granddaughters and a grandson.

Life after Bristol Rovers
SECOND SERIES

MARK LEESDAD

redcliffe

First published in 2009 by Redcliffe Press Ltd.,
81g Pembroke Road, Bristol BS8 3EA

www.redcliffepress.co.uk
info@redcliffepress.co.uk

© Mark Leesdad

ISBN   978-1-906593-09-4

British Library Cataloguing-in-Publication Data
A catalogue record for this book is available from the British Library

All rights reserved. Except for the purpose of review, no part of this book may be reproduced, stored in a retrieval system, or transmitted, in any form or by any means, electronic, mechanical, photocopying, recording or otherwise, without the prior permission of the publishers.

Design and typesetting by Steve Leary, steve@stevedesign.plus.com
Printed by HSW Print, Tonypandy, Rhondda

Contents

Acknowledgements	6		
Introduction	7		
Julian Alsop	8	Ronnie Mauge	68
Bruce Bannister	10	Christian McClean	70
Jon Bass	12	Jeff Meacham	72
Aidy Boothroyd	14	Michael Meaker	74
Martyn Britten	16	Don Megson	76
Trevor Challis	18	Kevin Miller	78
Andy Collett	20	Trevor Morgan	80
Steve Cross	22	Paul Nixon	82
Ian Davies	24	Malcolm Norman	84
Mike Davis	26	Mark O'Connor	86
Jim Eadie	28	Lindsay Parsons	88
Gary Emmanuel	30	Martin Paul	90
Gordon Fearnley	32	Shaun Penny	92
Jon French	34	Nick Platnauer	94
Ali Gibb	36	Frankie Prince	96
Carl Gilbert	38	Tom Ramasut	98
Dave Gilroy	40	John Rudge	100
Mike Green	42	Robbie Ryan	102
Ron Green	44	Dave Savage	104
Andy Gurney	46	John Scales	106
Steve Harding	48	Justin Skinner	108
Paul Hardyman	50	Gary Smart	110
Peter Higgins	52	Robin Stubbs	112
David Hillier	54	John Taylor	114
Scott Howie	56	Gary Waddock	116
Graham Hyde	58	Alan Warboys	118
Wayne Jones	60	Brian Williams	120
Gavin Kelly	62	David Williams	122
Larry Lloyd	64	Geraint Williams	124
Lee Maddison	66	Johnny Williams	126

Acknowledgements

Oh dear – that dreaded moment in print where you have to say 'thank you.' Sure as not, you're bound to leave someone out you should have mentioned or else offend somebody who thinks that they ought to have been given a name check.

As in volume one of *Life After Bristol Rovers*, my thanks again to my former bosses Christine Foster, Bill Edwardes and Richard Smith for all their help and guidance, as I turned to 'wordsmithing' as a career.

On the picture front I am once again indebted to photographer and good friend Phil McCheyne of Nailsea (www.philmccheynephoto.com). I have worked with Phil for a number of years now, been on hundreds of photo-shoots with him and rate him highly, which is why a number of the modern-day photos in this book are his work.

As far as many of the playing-days photos are concerned, I must thank Bristol Rovers historian Mike Jay, who has loaned me countless photographs from his personal collection, many taken by Rovers photographer Alan Marshall. Mike has also helped tremendously with biographical details in a lot of cases. I owe you one Mike. Also, to various newspapers and photographers around the country who have let me use photographic material, my thanks (credits as shown).

Ever conscious of copyright, I have not used any photos carrying a copyright stamp without permission.

I must also acknowledge everyone at Bristol Rovers (particularly Ian Holtby) for all their help and unreserved cooperation.

In terms of thanks, I can't let the occasion pass without a mention for *The Sunday Independent* and their sports supremo John Collings (JC) who gave me the go-ahead to write my weekly Memory Lane series, ultimately leading to the idea being translated into book format.

Special thanks for their faith in this project must also go my publishers, Bristol-based Redcliffe Press, experts in this field of work and renowned local publishers – a good combination.

And finally: to all those former players who gave up their time, dug up old photos and news cuttings and welcomed me into their homes or places of work to be asked a million questions, my eternal thanks. Without their help, cooperation and patience, this book wouldn't exist.

Mark Leesdad

PS – And thank you for buying this book.

Introduction

Many things have been said and written about Bristol Rovers, but one thing is very true – life as a 'Gashead' player or supporter is never dull. Memories of that lovely old Eastville 'gas flavoured' stadium; the infamous bribery scandal of the early sixties (you won't find Esmond Million or Keith Williams in this book); the 'temporary' stay at Bath City; the return to Bristol and, more recently, the on-off redevelopment of the Memorial Stadium. Never a dull moment.

And with all this talk of the club's history, the most important piece of the jigsaw – the players. What became of them after life as a Pirate? Well, as in volume one of *Life After Bristol Rovers*, I've continued to track down those players who wore the Rovers blue and white, both for my column in *The Sunday Independent* and for this book.

Why a second volume? Well, players continue to come and go. Some stay in the game, precarious though coaching and management is, while others seek a new challenge. And, having written about many Rovers stalwarts in the first book, more have since been tracked down – hence the second series.

I'm sure that there are still more ups-and-downs to come on the roller coaster that is Bristol Rovers, but in the meantime, I hope you enjoy this new offering.

JULIAN ALSOP

Ask most football managers where they start in building a team and most will probably say getting the right goalkeeper, centre half and centre forward – the spine of the side – will lay the foundations of putting together a good team. So it should come as no surprise that back in 1997, Bristol Rovers brought in former brickie Julian Alsop to spearhead their attack.

'At the time I was playing non-league football for Halesowen Town and working on a building site in Nuneaton,' said Julian. 'I had a pretty good scoring record at that level, but at twenty-three, I'd thought the chance of full-time football had passed me by.'

Geoff Twentyman was the Rovers' man who'd been watching Julian, or 'Jools' as he is known to his team mates, and it was on his recommendation that manager Ian Holloway signed the bustling six-foot-four striker, with Halesowen receiving a fee of £15,000.

'I don't think Ollie actually saw me play before signing me,' confessed Julian. 'I met him on the Thursday night, signed for the club, trained on the Friday and was on the bench for the first team on the Saturday.' And the job on the building site? 'I packed that in the minute Rovers offered me a three-year contract,' he replied with a smile.

Julian came on as a sub in that first game, a 4-2 win against Luton Town at The Memorial Ground. 'It was a dream come true to step up to professional football, but the first thing I found was how hard and intense the training was, compared to what I had been used to,' he admitted. 'Also, as you would expect, the players I was playing with – Andy Tillson, Peter Beadle, Justin Skinner and Jamie Cureton, to name just a few – were far more skilful than what I'd been used to.'

He went on to play around 40 first-team games for Rovers, scoring four league goals. 'I always gave one hundred per cent when I played and I think the Rovers fans appreciated that,' he said.

In 1998 Julian moved on to Swansea, initially on loan, before they paid Rovers £30,000 for his transfer – Rovers making a 100 per cent profit on their original outlay. He went on to make nearly a century of appearances for 'The Swans', scoring 16 goals.

But it was his next move, to Cheltenham Town, that really proved to be the landmark of his career. Striking up a wonderful partnership up front with the diminutive Tony Naylor (a case of 'Little and Large') Julian netted 35 goals, including 26 in one season and the second goal in the 3-1 Division Three Play Off Final win over Rushden & Diamonds.

In 2003 Julian moved to Oxford, playing around 40 games, but a training ground incident saw him sacked by the club and suspended from football. Short spells followed at Northampton Town, Tamworth, Forest Green Rovers (twice), Newport County and Cirencester, before Julian signed for his present club, Bishops Cleeve, who play in the British Gas Business Southern League Division One (South & West).

Away from football, Julian attended the University of Gloucester, where he studied accounting and financial management. He lives in Cheltenham with his wife Katherine and the couple have two young daughters – Lucy and Molly Mae.

Julian during his Bristol Rovers days.

Julian Alsop today.

BRUCE BANNISTER

Back in the seventies there were some great double acts. Morecambe & Wise, Starsky & Hutch and, the best of all if you happened to live in the blue half of Bristol, Smash & Grab – aka Alan Warboys and Bruce Bannister. The striking duo scored over 150 goals for The Pirates and formed one of the deadliest partnerships around.

'Alan and I struck up an understanding early on and once the goals started going in the 'Smash and Grab' thing started,' said Bruce.

Born in Bradford, Bruce was on Leeds United's books as a schoolboy, but switched to Bradford City to be nearer home. 'I got into the first team when I was seventeen,' recalled Bruce. 'I played alongside some very good players there – Tony Leighton, Bobby Ham, John Hall, and Kenny Leek, to name just a few.'

Over the years, many of Bruce's goals – he scored over 200 – came from the penalty spot. 'When I first joined the club, Charlie Rackstraw was the penalty taker. I don't think he ever missed one. We used to stay behind after training, practising spot kicks and I took over the role when Charlie left.'

In 1971, after over 200 games and 58 goals for 'The Bantams', Bruce was transferred to Bristol Rovers. And so began a love affair with the club and fans that was to last five years, see Bruce net 93 goals and have his name entered into Rovers' folklore. 'I hit a rich scoring vein early on, which is always handy when you move to a new club.'

It got even better for him two years later when Alan Warboys arrived and they combined up front to form the deadliest of striking partnerships, resulting in promotion from the Third Division and one game in particular that will remain in the memories of Rovers fans of a certain age. Brighton & Hove Albion 2 Bristol Rovers 8.

'We were on an unbeaten run when we went to Brighton. Cloughie had just taken over there and, because so many games had been cancelled because of the bad weather, the ground was packed with fans and also the national media – including the TV people,' recalled Bruce.

On a frozen pitch, Clough's Brighton side was hammered, Bruce scoring three and Alan Warboys four. 'To say Mister Clough wasn't very happy would be something of an understatement,' said Bruce with a smile.

But, of course, all good things come to an end and the Smash and Grab duo was broken up. Bruce left for Plymouth Argyle in 1976 and Warboys for Fulham a year later.

'Tony Waiters was the Argyle manager and the reason I went there,' revealed Bruce. 'When he got the push I didn't want to stay.' Not that Mrs Bannister was too pleased with Bruce's decision. 'We originally stayed in a hotel, then got our own place. My wife Janet had just finished hanging up the new curtains when I got a move to Hull City.'

And so, less than a year after joining Plymouth, Bruce was on his way to Hull, where he was to enjoy two and a half seasons, before finishing his professional career playing in France for Union Sportive Dunkirk.

After he finished playing Bruce started his own sportswear company. He now has a thriving business employing around 50 staff, including son Brett and daughter Victoria, selling all types of sports shoes, plus other sportswear and equipment on-line worldwide.

Bruce, on the ball for Rovers.

Bruce Bannister the business man.

JON BASS

Weston-born Jon Bass certainly went the long way round, before signing for a club right on his doorstep. In order to make the 25-mile trip to The Memorial Ground, Jon came via Malaysia. Throw in spells at Birmingham, Carlisle, Gillingham and Hartlepool, and Jon had certainly clocked up the miles to 'come home'.

'I used to play for Milton Nomads in Weston as a youngster and joined Birmingham City, then managed by Terry Cooper, as a sixteen-year-old,' said Jon, who lives in the Clifton area of Bristol with his partner Katy.

A boardroom take over and a change of manager saw Jon make his first-team debut in the 1994/95 season. 'I played my first game against Blackburn Rovers, marking winger Jason Wilcox and he soon let me know he was there with a few dodgy tackles,' recalled Jon. 'Barry Fry was Birmingham's manager by then – what a character he was.'

After a spell on the injured list with ruptured knee ligaments, Jon regained his first-team place, with local legend Trevor Francis in the manager's hot seat. 'Trevor was a bit aloof, but I'll always be grateful to him for giving me most of my first-team games there,' pointed out Jon, who also had a short loan spell at Carlisle.

Apart from three league games for Carlisle, Jon also had a loan spell at Gillingham, towards the end of the 2000/1 season. 'I enjoyed it there. The team was playing well and won promotion and the manager, Peter Taylor, had indicated he wanted to make my move permanent.' But the move fell through when Taylor went to Leicester.

Returning to the Midlands, Jon finally clocked up around 80 senior appearances for Birmingham, before being released at the end of the 2000/1 season. Next stop for Jon was one of soccer's outposts – Hartlepool United. 'I had two-and-a-half years there and helped the team get promotion from League Two,' he said.

But injuries at Victoria Park restricted Jon to 27 senior appearances, although he did score his one and only league goal there. 'People always bring up the fact that I only got one goal,' said Jon with a laugh. 'Good goal though – a header from the edge of the box.'

'When Hartlepool let me go I was weighing up my options, when my agent got in touch to say Pahang, a club side in Kuantan on the east coast of Malaysia, were interested in signing me, so I packed my bags and went,' said Jon, who was an ever present as the team won the Malaysian Premier League.

But, after a year away, Jon decided he wanted to be back in England. An invitation by Ian Atkins for him to train with Rovers was gratefully accepted and subsequently led to short-term contracts with The Pirates. 'I enjoyed it at Rovers and desperately wanted to do well for the fans, who were terrific,' said Jon. But, after around a dozen games, Jon decided to step down from full-time soccer, took an Open University course and obtained a BSc (Hons) in economics.

'I've been playing part-time for Salisbury and working as a quantity surveyor. I enjoyed my time as a pro, but after fourteen years and a lot of miles, I'm happy with my life.'

Jon in his Rovers days.

Busy at work, Jon today.

AIDY BOOTHROYD

Having honed his coaching skills at Peterborough United, Norwich City, West Brom and Leeds United, Aidy Boothroyd was the surprise choice to manage Watford in 2005. But any doubts the critics had were silenced when he took the club from the foot of the Championship to promotion to the Premiership. Sadly, when the club had a bad run of results in the 2008/9 season, Aidy paid the inevitable price.

Of course, long before Aidy had started to make his mark in coaching and management, he had cut his teeth as a player with four clubs, including Bristol Rovers.

'I started out with Huddersfield and played about a dozen games for them, including a one-all draw with Rovers at Huddersfield,' pointed out Aidy. A useful defender, Aidy's display had obviously caught the eye of Rovers management, with a view to being a future signing. 'Gerry Francis brought me to Bristol, before he moved on,' said Aidy. Following Gerry's departure, the Rovers' office seemed to have a revolving door, with Aidy serving under Martin Dobson, Dennis Rofe and Malcolm Allison. 'Interesting times!' said Aidy.

'Bristol was a good experience. There was a great team spirit in the club. I lived in Keynsham and Brislington during my two-and-a-half years there. The only trouble was that most of the time I was understudy to 'Jocky' Alexander and the so-and-so played brilliantly every week and rarely got injured!'

With just 16 league appearances in Rovers colours, Aidy moved north, signing for Scottish club Hearts. 'I loved Edinburgh, it's a lovely part of the world. I even scored a couple of goals for them, including the Scottish 'goal of the season' – and I wasn't renowned for my goalscoring.'

After Hearts, Aidy moved to Mansfield, where he was to enjoy the most consistent spell of his playing career, notching up over 200 games for 'The Stags'. 'I have to say that it was the most enjoyable time of my playing days in terms of first-team football.'

In 1996 Aidy moved up a division, signing for Barry Fry's Peterborough United. 'I played around thirty games for 'The Posh' but then suffered a broken leg break at Notts County,' revealed Aidy. The break was a bad one. So bad that, at the age of 26, Aidy had to give up playing. 'It was a sad day for English football when I had to retire!' he joked.

'After the injury I wanted to stay in the game and was given a coaching role at Peterborough, looking after the youngsters,' continued Aidy, who later moved on to become youth team coach at Norwich. By then, his skills and new ideas as a coach had earned him a good reputation in the game and, after two-and-a-half years at Carrow Road, he went to West Bromwich Albion as youth development officer and technical director. Later, he took up the post of first team coach at Leeds United.

In March 2005 Aidy was offered the manager's job at Watford, where he went on to achieve the unthinkable – promotion via the Play Offs, to the top tier of English football.

'I've worked with and played for some of the biggest names in football and I'd like to think I've learnt something from all of them. In fact, I'm a thief, I've taken on board the best of all of them.'

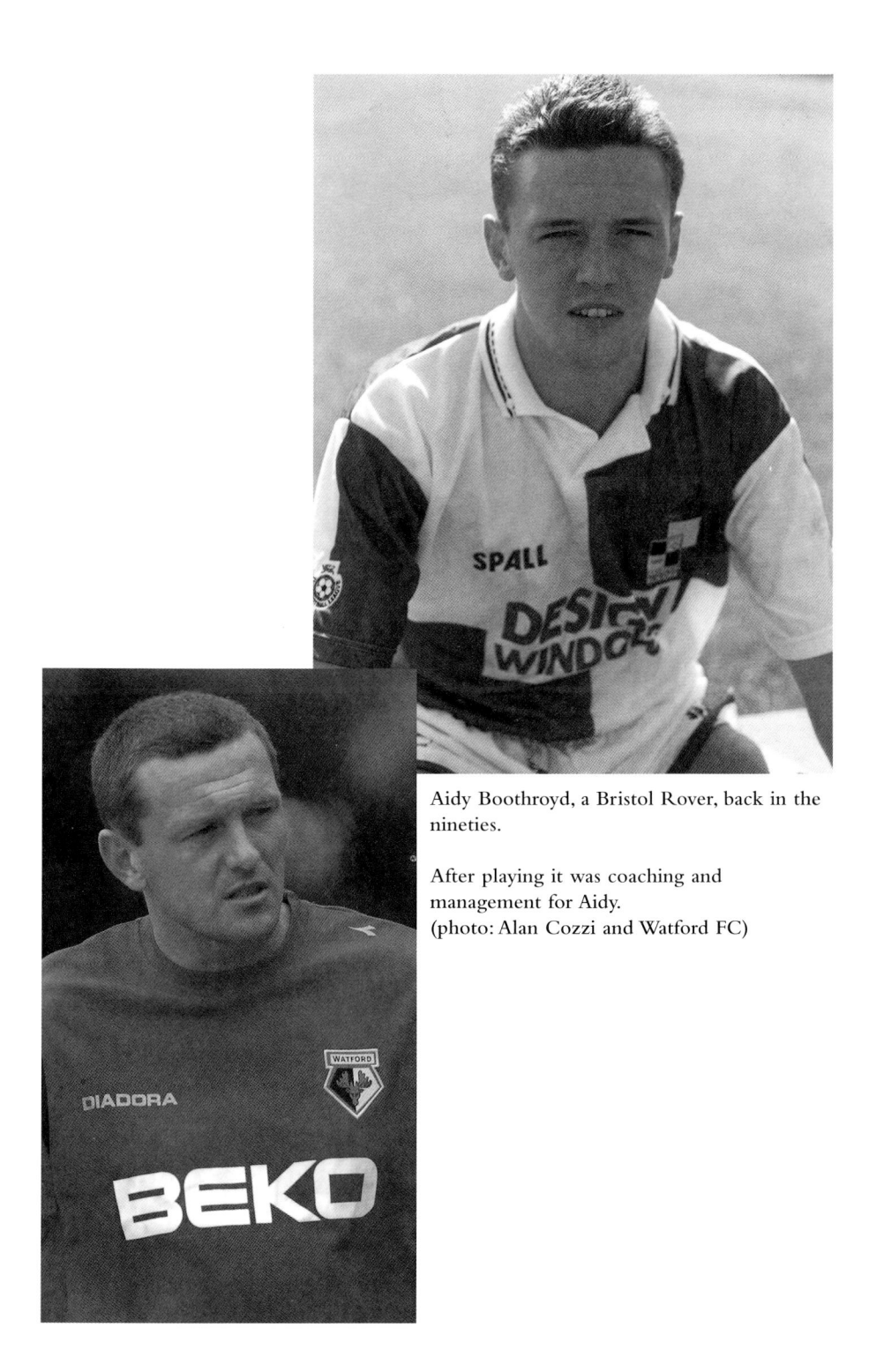

Aidy Boothroyd, a Bristol Rover, back in the nineties.

After playing it was coaching and management for Aidy.
(photo: Alan Cozzi and Watford FC)

MARTYN BRITTEN

'Call me old fashioned, but I think Bristol Rovers lost some of their magic when they left Eastville. To me it was their spiritual home and I've not been back since a certain furniture store was built on the ground.' So says former Rovers winger Martyn Britten.

A member of the Bristol Boys team, Martyn was originally going to sign for big rivals City as a youngster. 'Bobby Campbell, who was a coach at Rovers at the time, took the Bristol Boys team for training and thought I had potential. He recommended me to manager Bill Dodgin who came and watched me and, after checking that I hadn't actually signed for City, signed me on schoolboy forms,' explained Martyn.

Martyn progressed and at 16 became an apprentice professional. He went on to sign as a full-time pro, along with fellow apprentices Peter Aitken, Phil Bater and Richard Crabtree. Like most former players, he vividly recalls his senior debut. 'It was in the old Second Division against Bolton Wanderers. I was being marked by a full back called Don McAllister, who was sold to Spurs for big money not long after. I must have done OK as I ended getting the man of the match award.'

Despite his good start and a 2-1 win for Rovers, Martyn was left out of the side for the next game, making a total of just three appearances in that season – 1974/5. The following year, though, he had 14 league games to his credit and two goals. 'One of those was a header [against Luton Town] which surprised everyone, including me, as heading was never my strongest asset,' he said with a smile.

Big crowds were quite common at Eastville in those days, with Martyn playing in a goalless draw against arch rivals City, which drew over 26,000 to the ground for the Second Division fixture. Something else that was quite common at that time, was back-to-back fixtures over the Bank Holidays, with Rovers playing three games in four days over that Easter period. 'We were home again the day after the City match, taking on a Southampton side that included Peter Osgood, Alan Ball, Nick Holmes and Mick Channon,' recalled Martyn. 'We beat them two-nil, which was very good considering the star players they had. And don't forget, this was the same Southampton side that went on to beat Manchester United in the Cup Final.'

Although Martyn was to notch up 14 games that season, the following year he was restricted to just three league appearances. 'I had the chance of a loan move to America, but the club refused to let me go. Then, after the chance had gone and the season was over, I found I wasn't being retained.'

In the summer of 1977 Martyn moved on, signing for Reading, but a broken ankle brought about the end of his career as a professional footballer.

After leaving Reading, Martyn had a season with local non-league side Taunton Town, before quitting soccer altogether – although he later turned out for Glastonbury. Conscious of the need to have a trade, Martyn had been working as a builder for his former father-in-law. He retrained to learn all the necessary skills and now runs his own building firm.

Married to Victoria, Martyn has two children from his first marriage.

Martyn, second from the left, middle row.

Now a successful builder, Martyn Britten at work today.

TREVOR CHALLIS

If things had worked out differently, self-confessed Arsenal fan Trevor Challis might have been part of 'The Gunners' success story. Instead, he decided that there were better opportunities at Queens Park Rangers, before making his mark with five seasons and 172 games with Bristol Rovers.

'Arsenal were 'my team' and I was on their books at fourteen-years-old and went to their Centre of Excellence,' revealed Trevor. 'Later I decided I had more chance of making the break through with QPR and went to Loftus Road.

'I made my senior debut against Everton, marking Andre Kanchelskis, what a player,' recalled Trevor. 'Later I played against my heroes at Arsenal and was detailed to mark Dennis Bergkamp. He certainly gave me the run-around and taught me a few lessons that day!'

Trevor's progress with QPR was halted when he suffered a bad knee injury. 'I was out for nineteen months and had four operations,' said Trevor. By the time he had recovered, he was unable to force his way back into the team and, with just 15 league games with QPR, was looking for another club.

'Ollie, who knew me from his time at Queens Park Rangers, brought me to Bristol. They already had Matt Lockwood and Graeme Power from QPR, so there were some familiar faces already there.'

That was in the summer of '98 and Trevor went on to establish himself as a regular in The Pirates defence, notching up 172 appearances and scoring one goal. 'Ah, my one and only goal,' said Trevor with a smile. 'It was a top-of-the-table clash with Wigan and we were losing one-nil. Nathan Ellington got a cross in and I caught it on the edge of the box and let fly. I think it took a deflection on the way in, but it was my goal all the way.'

During his five seasons with Rovers, Trevor played for four managers. What did he think of them? 'Ollie was very passionate about the club, perhaps too passionate. He was Bristol Rovers 'twenty-four seven' and sometimes you need to be able to switch off and step back. Gary Thompson was a bit hard done by and not given enough time and, although I have the utmost respect for him, it didn't really work for Gerry [Francis] when he came back a second time.' And Ray Graydon? 'It's a shame when a former player who has done so well comes back to manage and it goes wrong. Things just didn't work under his management and I didn't enjoy playing for him.'

It was during the ill-fated reign of Ray Graydon that Trevor left Rovers after 'three good seasons and two write-offs' and joined the seemingly ambitious non league club Telford United. 'We were doing OK and then the money ran out and the club went bust,' recalled Trevor.

After Telford, Trevor went to Shrewsbury, playing a key role in their reclaiming league status, after netting the deciding penalty that won them promotion out of the Conference. After 16 months he went to Weymouth, where he spent three years and also ran the youth set up. These days he plays for Blue Square South club Eastleigh.

Very much involved in youth coaching, Trevor is taking all the necessary courses to obtain his coaching badges. Married to hairdresser Sally, the couple live in the Emerson Green area of Bristol and have a young daughter, Isabella.

Trevor in action.

Swotting up for his coaching badges.

ANDY COLLETT

You can always tell just how well a player is thought of by the reception he gets after he's moved on and returns to his old club, playing for the opposition. Former goalkeeper Andy Collett remembers with affection the reaction he got from Rovers fans, when he returned to play against them for his new club, Darlington.

'I've played at The Mem twice with 'Darlo' and got a fantastic reception on both occasions,' he recalled. 'Rovers fans are the most loyal I've ever come across and that reception meant a great deal to me.'

A northern lad born in Stockton, Andy started out on soccer's long and winding road when he signed schoolboy forms for Middlesbrough. 'I was thirteen at the time and Boro had spotted me playing local schools football,' he said. But, with Stephen Pears and Allan Miller ahead of him in the pecking order, Andy was restricted to just seven first team appearances and, eager for first team football, left the club at 21.

'I came down to Rovers originally on loan,' said Andy. 'I found there was a great team spirit at the club, the fans were fantastic and the manager, John Ward, was top class, so I was happy to sign on the dotted line once the clubs had agreed a fee.'

Andy was to spend five seasons with Rovers and struck up a rapport with the supporters, always taking time out for a chat or to sign autographs, once the game was over. 'I think it's only right and proper to find time for the fans. They pay a lot of money to watch you play and are due respect,' he pointed out. He lists winning a Player of the Year award as one of his fondest memories of his time at Rovers.

In 1999 Andy moved back to the north, signing for Darlington and quickly became as much a favourite with their fans as he did with the 'Gasheads.' He helped his new club reach the Play Offs in his first season and also picked up another Player of the Year awards to match the one he got at Rovers.

After four seasons keeping goal for 'The Quakers' Andy was forced to call it a day, after suffering a broken shoulder. Not that he left the soccer scene altogether. After finishing his playing career, he took up a position as goalkeeping coach at the club, passing on the benefits of his skills and experience to the side's shot stoppers.

Andy held this post for five years, before taking up a similar position with Oldham Athletic at the end of last season.

Married to Kerry, the couple have a young daughter (Lily) and baby son (Henry).

Andy Collett when he was Rovers' keeper.

After his playing days Andy became Darlington's goalkeeping coach.
(photo: *The Northern Echo*)

STEVE CROSS

When Bristol Rovers signed Derby's Steve Cross in 1991, he'd played at some of the best grounds in the country. During his six seasons with 'The Rams' he'd been used to playing on top-class pitches, with great spectator amenities and luxury dressing rooms. Then he came to Twerton Park!

Born in Wolverhampton, Steve wrote to practically every club in The Midlands asking for a trial when he left school. 'I got an invite to go along to Shrewsbury Town, was given an apprenticeship and made the first team at seventeen,' he recalled. 'I played some three hundred games for them, mostly in the old Second Division and have very fond memories of my time at the club.'

In 1986, Steve was transferred to Derby County, going on to win promotion to the top flight in his first season. 'I played around eighty games for Derby, but in my last season rarely featured, as I had been out injured. When I'd recovered, the manager was very honest with me and told me my first-team appearances would probably be limited.'

Enter Bristol Rovers. 'I was told Rovers were in for me and I met Martin Dobson and ended up signing without seeing the ground. It was a bit of a shock. Mind you, there weren't many teams who enjoyed coming to Twerton Park and it became known as Fortress Twerton.'

It was while he was still finding his feet at Bath that Steve had another shock – the sacking of the man who signed him. 'I think I'd only been there about six weeks when Martin got the bullet.' Dennis Rofe took over, before Malcolm Allison was brought in to 'help' the manager, ultimately leading to Rofe's departure.

Steve went on to make 43 appearances for Rovers but, by the time Allison had left, Steve was already involved in coaching. 'I had three years coaching and playing in the reserves, before stepping up to assistant manager. When Malcolm left I was put in charge for three games, prior to John Ward coming in.'

Ward's appointment was too late to prevent relegation to soccer's third tier. But, during his three years in charge at Rovers, assisted by Steve, he took the club to the Southern Area Final of the Auto Windscreen Shield and also the Play Offs. But board room politics came into play and Ward was sacked. 'I think they made a big mistake getting rid of John,' said Steve. 'To complicate things, I'd just signed a new two-year contract. 'Ollie' took over as player-manager and said he wanted to bring in his own coaching staff. I could see he felt awkward about the situation, so I made it easy for him and said I'd leave.

'After that I went to South Bristol College and took my A Levels in health studies and put my boots back on to play for Mangotsfield. Later I went back to Twerton Park to play for Bath City.'

After South Bristol College, Steve attended Birmingham University to take a course in health and podiatry-related issues, before joining Social Services to help adults with learning difficulties. He now works as a physio for Telford Hospital and is also a commentator at Shrewsbury matches for local radio.

Married to Helen, the couple have two sons and live in Shrewsbury.

A young Steve Cross (centre) celebrates a goal for Shrewsbury Town.
(photo: *Shrewsbury Chronicle & Journal Series*)

Match commentator Steve Cross today.

IAN DAVIES

Bristol-born Ian Davies certainly took the long route to sign for one of his local clubs – Bristol Rovers. He came via Norwich, Newcastle, Manchester, Bury, Brentford, Cambridge, Carlisle, Exeter and Yeovil. Throw in a spell playing in The States and that's quite a few miles before winding up at the city you were born in.

'I joined Norwich as an apprentice,' said Ian. 'Not long afterwards I made my first-team debut, when I came on as a sub in a First Division game against Birmingham.' In fact, Ian was 'The Canaries' youngest ever debutant at just 17 years and 29 days old.

During his time at Carrow Road, Ian played 32 league games, scoring two goals. 'Getting into the first team was great. I played at some of the biggest grounds in the country – White Hart Lane, Old Trafford, Highbury – and played against some great wingers.' Ian also played for the Welsh Under-23 team and enjoyed a loan spell with Detroit Express in America. 'That was a fantastic experience. I was just twenty-one and there I was, flying everywhere and playing against the likes of Franz Beckenbauer. The manager of the team was Ken Furphy and I have to say he's probably the best manager I've ever played under.'

Back home, Ian left Norwich in 1979, a £150,000 transfer fee taking him to Newcastle United. Predominantly a left back, he went on to notch up over 70 league appearances for 'The Magpies', scoring three times. In 1982 Ian was reunited with former Norwich boss John Bond at Manchester City, but played just a handful of games for the (then) Maine Road side, having loan spells at Bury, Brentford and Cambridge, plus short periods at Carlisle, Exeter and Yeovil, before 'coming home' to sign for Rovers in August 1985.

Ian made his Rovers debut against Darlington, keeping his place for the following game, when he scored in a 3-2 defeat at Reading. 'There were some good players on the books when I came to Rovers,' recalled Ian. 'Ron Green was dependable in goal, Timmy Parkin was a steady centre half, Mark O'Connor was a useful winger, Steve White up front, a very under-rated player, and Paul Randall, a natural goal scorer.

'The trouble was I was on monthly contracts at Rovers and while the manager [Bobby Gould] kept talking about getting me on a full contract, it just didn't happen,' pointed out Ian. 'I was a regular in the squad, but the promise of a full-time contract just didn't materialize.'

And so, after 14 league appearances and less than four months after joining The Pirates, Ian moved on, signing for Swansea. But a late tackle was to spell the end to any hopes Ian had of a long career with 'The Swans'. 'I played about a dozen games for Swansea. We were playing Doncaster Rovers and one of their lads came in late and I ended up with a broken leg and that spelt the end,' said Ian.

After football, Ian worked for a hardware company for a while, before taking up delivery driving. These days he works for a logistics company, delivering mainly medical supplies. Married to Julie, the couple live in Nailsea and have two grown-up sons.

Ian in his playing days.

Ian today.

MIKE DAVIS

Former Pirate Mike Davis is unlikely to forget his senior baptism for Bristol Rovers. It was at the old Den, home of Millwall, and was the last game played there. 'There was a full house, there were pitch invasions before, during and after the match, the fans were dismantling bits of the stadium as souvenirs and every time the ball went into the crowd, they refused to throw it back!' recalled Mike. 'Add to that the fact that we won and I scored the last-ever goal at the ground and it's not a game I'm likely to forget.'

Mike's Millwall debut was in stark contrast to what he had been used to, prior to joining Rovers. 'I had been playing local non-league football in front of around 200 people – and that was on a good day,' he pointed out.

A member of the Avon Schools side as a youngster, Mike caught Rovers' eye after scoring 40 goals for Yate's youth team. A natural striker, until reverting to defender later in his career, Mike faced a stiff challenge to get into Rovers' first team. 'When you think that during my two years with Rovers, they had the likes of Marcus Stewart, Peter Beadle, Martin Paul, John Taylor, Paul Miller, Carl Saunders and Gareth Taylor there, it was never going to easy to get in the side,' admitted Mike.

In addition to the competition for places, Mike was also unlucky with injuries. 'I had a bad ankle injury, which kept me on the sidelines for over eight weeks and then, when I got back into the first team, I injured my other ankle against Spurs.'

Although first-team opportunities were limited, Mike had nothing but praise for the set-up at Rovers. 'John Ward was an excellent manager, very thorough,' he said. 'And in Dennis Booth and Terry Connor he had two of the best coaches I ever worked with.'

After two years with Rovers, with Mike making 17 first team appearances and scoring twice, he moved on to Bath City, where he came into his own. He went on to make over 250 senior appearances for 'The Romans', netting nearly a century of goals. 'I loved my time at Bath,' said Mike, who regularly topped the scoring charts, before switching to a wing-back position. But after five years at Twerton, Mike moved on to Basingstoke.

'I felt it was time for a change, but the move proved to me that the grass certainly isn't greener elsewhere,' he admitted. Unsettled at Basingstoke, Mike returned for a month's loan spell at Twerton, before joining Mangotsfield. 'After a season with Mangotsfield, I played for Cirencester for a year and a half. I got my confidence and form back and enjoyed it there,' said Mike. Then it was back to his roots, as Mike returned to Yate Town, where he enjoyed two more seasons. 'My career had definitely gone full cycle.'

Away from soccer, Mike worked in the health and leisure industry for a while, before switching to the timber industry as an internal salesman. Living in Crudwell, just outside Malmesbury, Mike is married to Sarah and the couple have a young daughter – Grace.

'Looking back at that Millwall game, it seems like a lifetime ago, but one match I will never forget – very scary,' said Mike. 'In fact, I'm still having therapy treatment!' he added with a laugh.

Mike in footballing action.

Mike at work.

JIM EADIE

If a City and a Rovers supporter were having a discussion back at the start of the 73/74 season and the Rovers fan said that his team would get promotion, it would not have been unusual for a City fan to respond 'yes – and pigs might fly!' Well Rovers did get promotion that season and a 'pig' did fly. For Rovers goalkeeper was a certain Jim Eadie, who had been given the somewhat irreverent, but affectionate, nickname 'The Flying Pig.'

'Rovers going up was definitely one of the very best moments of my career,' said Jim. And, despite the nickname, Jim's speed and agility between the sticks played a huge part in the Bristol Rovers success that year.

Born in Alexandria in Scotland – a caber's toss from beautiful Loch Lomond – Jim played for Scottish junior team Kirkintiloch Rob Roy. He went on to join Glasgow Rangers as a youth player and later appeared in the first team for both Dumbarton and Forfar Athletic.

'I came down south for a trial with Leicester City,' said Jim, his broad Scottish accent hardly dented by many years living over the border. 'Of course, when I got there I found they already had two pretty decent keepers on their books – Gordon Banks and Peter Shilton!' And Jim's luck was right out, as he suffered an ankle injury during the trial.

Undeterred, Jim returned to Scotland, but it wasn't long before he was again under the scrutiny of the scouts, resulting in a move to Cardiff City. 'Cardiff were top of the old Second Division at the time and, towards the end of the season, we only needed one win from our last three games to go up to the top division,' explained Jim. Sadly for all at Cardiff, they blew it and missed out.

In February 1973, after a short loan-spell at Chester, Jim came to Eastville, to take over from the injured Dick Sheppard in Rovers goal. His first game saw him in top form, as Rovers ground out a nil-nil draw at Blackburn. Proving that his display wasn't a one-off, Jim went on to keep clean sheets in Rovers' next four games.

The following season, Rovers swept all before them to win promotion, with Jim totting up around 700 minutes between the sticks without letting a goal in – a huge factor in Rovers' success.

Over the next three seasons Jim missed just three games, but, at the end of the 76/77 season, he left the club. 'It was a contractual dispute,' explained Jim. 'I only wanted another fiver a week, but the club wouldn't budge, so I upped and left.'

A season playing at Bath City under Brian Godfrey followed – 'he still owes me a week's wages!'– with Jim playing part-time and working first in the building trade and later as a welder. But the years of diving about on a thousand football pitches had taken their toll and Jim was having problems with his back and knees.

Married to Michele, the couple live in the Kingswood area of Bristol and have seven children and four grandchildren. And the legacy of playing football is that Jim is on disability pension, has spinal disc problems and has undergone knee replacement surgery. 'So there's no chance of donning the keeper's jersey again?' 'More chance of pigs flying!' he replied with a smile.

Another training ground save from Jim Eadie.

Jim Eadie at home.

GARY EMMANUEL

Life was never dull when Gary Emmanuel was playing. His last season with Birmingham City saw the club relegated. In his second full season at Rovers they, too, were relegated and the main stand burnt down. His first season at Swindon also ended with relegation and a serious back injury saw him miss most of the season when he went to Newport. His last league club, Swansea City, was relegated and went bust. 'Just call me lucky!' said Gary.

Spotted by a Birmingham scout, Gary joined the club as a youngster in 1971. During his time there he made over 80 appearances, but spent a lot of time as a sub. 'I was on the bench so often I think I must have got splinters in my backside!' So when the chance of a move to Rovers, and regular first-team football, came about in December '78, he jumped at it.

'I loved it at Rovers. It was a nice part of the country, the supporters were very good and everyone was so friendly.' It was also home-from-home for Swansea-born Gary. 'There was a very strong Welsh contingent, with Tony Pulis, Vaughan Jones, Martin Thomas and David Williams, to name but a few,' he recalled.

Signed by Bobby Campbell, Gary went on to play under Harold Jarman and Terry Cooper in his two-and-a-half years with The Pirates, notching up over 70 appearances.

'The fire at Eastville was a body blow to everyone at the club and getting relegated at the end of that season made it a terrible year,' said Gary.

In the summer of '81, Gary moved up the road to Swindon Town. 'It was a good move because it meant we didn't have to move house,' pointed out Gary. Relegated to the (old) Fourth Division in his first year, Gary made over 100 appearances for Swindon, before moving back 'over the bridge' in 1984, when he signed for Newport County, then a Third Division side.

'I went to Newport on a year's contract, did my back in during pre-season and was out of the game for six months,' he revealed.

Released after just a dozen games for County, Gary had a trial with Lincoln City. 'They offered me a year's contract. The problem was they wanted me to move up there, so I turned it down.'

Gary followed that up with a short spell at Rovers' rivals, Bristol City. 'That was a disaster,' admitted Gary. 'I didn't get off to the best of starts. The fans were on my back because of the Rovers connection and I gave away a penalty on my home debut. It just wasn't working out and, with just three disastrous games behind me, I went to see Terry Cooper and had my contract cancelled by mutual consent.'

A move back home to Swansea seemed the perfect answer. 'It was a great move for me, but the club ran into serious financial difficulties and nearly went out of existence.'

Relegation at the end of that dramatic year was a little easier to take, given that the club had managed to recover from their financial problems. And, at least, Gary had some good luck for a change, when, in his last season with 'The Swans', the club won promotion.

Married to Lynne, the couple have a son and daughter and live in Swansea. Like so many former footballers, Gary is a postman.

Gary pictured during his time with Rovers.

Off to daughter Sarah's wedding: Gary and wife Lynne.

GORDON FEARNLEY

A former Gashead, Gordon Fearnley describes himself as something of 'an education junkie'. Certainly he's had to do his fair share of learning since leaving Eastville and Bristol Rovers. For, after finishing his playing days in the North American Soccer League, Gordon has been an attorney at law, a physiotherapist and a state registered nurse.

'It's the best way to get on in The States – education,' said Gordon. 'I graduated (Bsc) as a physiotherapist in 1985, before going to law school in '88, graduating three years later.'

But life as an attorney wasn't for Gordon. 'Actually, I enjoyed physiotherapy much more than trial litigation, so I quit the law profession after only one year and returned to nursing,' he explained.

Long before Bradford-born Gordon had thoughts of a new life in the USA, he had started out as a young professional with Sheffield Wednesday in the (old) First Division. After two years, often dogged by injury, Gordon came to Bristol, anxious to play first-team football, signing in July 1970. Also on Bristol Rovers books at the time was Wednesday legend Don Megson, who went on to manage Rovers from 1972 to 1977.

'Don had seen my injury-plagued time in Sheffield and was instrumental in setting me up with a two-month trial at Rovers,' recalled Gordon. 'It was a breath of fresh air to join a winning team with a positive attitude, after my last year with a relegated Sheffield Wednesday.'

After proving his fitness and ability, Gordon was offered a full contract. 'I worked my way up from the reserves into the first-team squad, spending much of my time coming off the subs' bench when things weren't going well. I think I played in every position in the front line, though I'd previously played purely as a centre forward.'

During his seven seasons with the club Gordon enjoyed Watney Cup success (Rovers beating Sheffield United on penalties in the final) and promotion from the old Third Division in a season that included that 8-2 thrashing of Brian Clough's Brighton at The Goldstone Ground. And, while Smash and Grab (aka Alan Warboys and Bruce Bannister) took the headlines by scoring seven of the goals between them, it was Gordon who got the other goal.

'We were playing exceptionally well at the time and felt we could dominate anyone. Don had put together a very good bunch of hard-working professionals and there was a great spirit in the dressing room.'

Gordon went on to complete close on 150 senior games for The Pirates, before the chance of a new challenge, playing in America, proved too good to turn down. 'A lot of English pros were joining the soccer revolution in The States and when I was approached to play for Miami Toros, I dug out my passport and went.'

After three seasons playing in Florida, Gordon spent two years as player/coach in Sacramento, California, and a final year playing in Chicago, before hanging up his boots and entering college.

'These days I combine therapy and nursing services to housebound patients who have had hip and/or knee replacement surgery here in the "Sunshine State".'

Married to Kathy, the couple live in South Florida.

Gordon in his Rovers days.

Enjoying life in The States, Gordon Fearnley today.

JON FRENCH

You start off as a young lad, dreaming of a life as a footballer. You join your local professional club as a trainee and you're on your way. So what's the worse that could happen? Well, breaking a leg right at the beginning of that dream would rate pretty highly in the catastrophe category. And that's exactly what happened to Jon French.

'At first they thought it was just a bad sprain,' said Jon. 'I went off for x-rays and even then it was six hours before they confirmed it was a fracture. I'd only been with the club ten days and was thinking my career was over before it had started.'

Jon was out of action for six months. 'In some ways it was a blessing in disguise, although I didn't think so at the time. I spent the time working with weights, swimming and concentrating on being ready physically and mentally once the break had healed.'

Once he was fully fit again, Jon restarted his career and soon earned a professional contract. 'I was doing OK and got about eighteen goals for the reserves, playing against teams such as Spurs and Arsenal, so it was a pretty high standard.'

It was in the 95/96 season that Rovers manager John Ward gave Jon his full first-team debut. 'It was against Peterborough at Twerton Park – we drew one all,' he recalled. He also remembered the two goals that he scored for Rovers. 'The first was a header against Cambridge United and the other was at Crewe.'

The following season, having featured a dozen or so times in the senior squad, Jon found himself loaned out to Conference side Bath City. 'It was a tough league to play in, but it was good experience,' said Jon, who finished on the losing side just once in 10 games.

Naturally disappointed to be released by Rovers at the end of the 96/97 season, Jon has nothing but praise for manager John Ward. 'A very good man-manager, an excellent football coach, I don't have a bad word to say about him.'

After trials at Woking and Plymouth Argyle, Jon was offered a contract by Hull City, then in the old Third Division. 'It was a long way from home, but that's part of pursuing a career as a footballer,' said Jon philosophically. But despite his determination, the move didn't work out. 'I played around twenty games for them, but I lost eight weeks with an ankle ligament injury, then they had a change of manager and I wasn't happy being a fringe player.'

A loan spell at Cheltenham came to nothing, before Jon signed for Welsh League side Barry Town. 'There were a lot of plusses playing for Barry. It was a good standard of football, the club was often involved in EUFA Cup and Champions League games and it was handy for Bristol,' said Jon, who had the distinction of scoring in a European Cup game for the team.

When the club ran into financial difficulties, though, Jon knew it was time to move on. 'I'd just bought a flat and had bills to pay,' he explained. 'I left and joined Weston-super-Mare and got a job at Bristol Airport.'

After playing for Weston, Jon joined Mangotsfield United in the Southern League. He later became joint caretaker manager there, before moving on to another Southern League side, Paulton Rovers.

A fitness and personal trainer, Jon lives in Portishead.

Jon during his Hull City days.

Working out at the gym.

ALI GIBB

When young footballers make the grade and have the chance to fulfill their dreams by becoming professionals, the chances are a lot of them probably don't give too much thought as to what they'll be doing when their professional playing days are over. Not so with former Rovers winger Ali Gibb, who was always conscious of the need to look at life after soccer, right from the start.

'I always knew that a career in football is relatively short-lived and was studying from the age of sixteen to make sure I was ready for the challenge of life after soccer,' said Ali, now working in financial planning with Barclays Bank in their Wales & West of England team.

Born in Salisbury, Ali was on Southampton's books as a youngster, but followed youth team manager Bob Higgins to Norwich. The chance of first-team football with a loan move to Northampton Town came in 1995 and he went on to spend five years with 'The Cobblers.'

'Northampton paid Norwich £30,000 to make the move permanent and I went on to play over 150 games for them, making the Play Offs two years running and winning promotion,' said Ali. 'Ian Atkins was the manager and it proved to be a successful period of my career.'

With his contract up, Ali accepted a new challenge by moving up two divisions to The Championship with Stockport County in a £50,000 transfer and spent five years at Edgeley Park, again adding another 150+ games to his cv, before moving to the South West and Bristol Rovers.

'I joined Rovers on transfer deadline day 2004, linking up again with Ian Atkins,' recalled Ali. 'Stockport wanted to reduce their wage bill and I asked to be released from my contract.'

And so Ali joined The Pirates, as they fought to avoid relegation to the Conference. 'Rovers had a great fan base and they were fantastic, even when the team was struggling,' said Ali.

With players coming and going as Atkins sought a winning team, it must have felt as if there were a revolving door at the home dressing room. 'When I made my debut I think there were six or seven new players in the line-up,' recalled Ali, who made a perfect start by scoring on his debut, one of two league goals he would score in his 64 senior appearances.

'Although there was a lot of coming and going, there were some very good players at the club, like Stuart Campbell, who is now Rovers skipper, and young Scott Sinclair.'

In the summer of 2006, with Atkins gone, Ali left for pastures new. 'Lennie Lawrence and Paul Trollope wanted to build their own team and I didn't have a problem with that,' said Ali, who joined Hartlepool United. He was to spend two years with Hartlepool, although the latter part was spent on loan at Notts County. 'After that I decided to make the break from full time football and embark on a career in finance. I had gained a number of qualifications through my extra-curricular studies [Ali has a degree in business and finance] and was in a position to exit the professional game.'

Although now engrossed in the world of finance, Ali has not given up football completely, having signed for Blue Square side Bath City last summer, although a pre-season injury meant he was side-lined for much of last season.

Ali, the professional footballer.

Another day in the world of financial matters for Ali Gibb.

CARL GILBERT

Dozens of players have been involved in various transfers en route to City and Rovers, but former Rovers' striker Carl Gilbert is probably the first Bristol player who started his professional soccer career with a transfer from Her Majesty's Forces.

'I joined the army at fifteen and was in the Royal Sussex Regiment based in Canterbury,' said Carl. A good all-round sportsman, Carl excelled at cricket, basketball, swimming, cross country and soccer. 'We got through to the quarter-finals of the army regimental cup and a coach from Gillingham came to give us some professional training, which is how I came to the attention of Gillingham Football Club,' explained Carl.

A guest appearance in Gillingham's youth team, together with the coach's recommendation, was enough to persuade 'The Gills' to pay out a 'transfer fee' to buy Carl out of the services and bring him into professional soccer.

'I played around fifty games for Gillingham, before Rovers expressed an interest in bringing me to Bristol,' continued Carl. With Rovers watching him in a reserve match at Bristol City, Carl certainly made an impression – getting sent off for violent conduct!

'That didn't deter Rovers' manager Bill Dodgin junior from signing me though – perhaps he was looking to add some punch to the attack!' he joked.

Carl signed for Rovers in January 1969, with Pirate Kenny Ronaldson going to Gillingham as part of the transfer. 'I loved my time at Bristol,' said Carl. 'We lived in Kingswood and our first child, Graham, was born there.'

During his two-year spell at Rovers, Carl played over 50 games for the club, scoring 15 league goals for them. 'There were some good players at Eastville at the time,' recalled Carl. 'Big Stuart Taylor at the back, Bobby Jones, Robin Stubbs and Ray Graydon – all good players and very good pals. Sadly, one of my best mates during my time there has passed on – Dick Sheppard, a lovely fellow and one of the best keepers I ever played with.'

In March 1971, Third Division rivals Rotherham United paid out £18,000 to take the blonde striker to Millmoor. Carl went on to make over 100 appearances for the club, scoring 36 league goals, including all four in a 4-nil win over Swansea. In July 1994, non league Margate paid out a record fee of £2,500 to secure his services. 'I could have stayed in the league at the time,' said Carl. 'York, Stockport and Doncaster offered me deals, but Margate was nearer home and the side had a lot of my old Gillingham team mates on the books.'

Carl had two seasons with Margate before moving on to Folkestone, where he played just 10 games, before suffering a broken leg. He tried his hand at management and coaching (with Canterbury City and, later, back at Folkestone) before calling it a day. He followed his father's footsteps in working on the railways, where he is now a contracts manager, assessor and instructor. 'The company is called Para Rail, which is ironic when you think I started with the Royal Sussex Regiment and finished up with the 'paras'!

Married to Joyce, the couple live in Folkestone and have two sons, Graham and Matthew, and a daughter – Katie. 'I've got a massive affection for the club and Rovers' is always the first result I look for,' summed up Carl.

Carl in his Bristol Rovers days.

A more recent photo of Carl.

DAVE GILROY

Former Bristol Rovers striker Dave Gilroy is a very hospitable sort of a bloke. Well he'd have to be, as he is events and sales executive for a local sporting hospitality company.

'The business was started in 1998 by former Gloucestershire County cricketer Andy Brassington,' said Dave. 'Basically we organize hospitality packages for soccer, rugby and cricket enthusiasts, including after-dinner speakers from the sporting world.'

Prior to getting into the hospitality business, Dave has been a professional footballer with Bristol Rovers. 'I joined Rovers on schoolboy forms and spent three years on the youth training scheme,' said Dave. 'I went on to become an apprentice and then had just over two years as a full-time pro.'

It was in August 2001 that Dave tasted first-team action, coming on as a substitute against Luton Town. He later made his full debut that same month against Darlington. 'Gerry Francis was manager at the time,' recalled Dave. 'He certainly knew his stuff and I shall always be grateful to him for giving me my big chance.'

Sadly, the club was struggling and Gerry's second spell in the manager's chair didn't work out as everyone had hoped. 'Gerry had come back to the club after we'd been relegated to the old Third Division. As well as trying to turn Rovers round, he was also having to deal with personal problems – two very close members of his family were very ill – and it resulted in his leaving.'

Gerry was followed into the manager's chair by Garry Thompson, but Rovers were a club on the slide and the nightmare of another relegation became a reality. The arrival of another former favourite, Ray Graydon, as team boss, did nothing to improve Rovers' fortunes.

Despite being a prolific scorer at youth and reserve level, Dave found it hard to reproduce his scoring form at first-team level. 'All strikers thrive on goals, but it's so much harder when the team is struggling and it hits your confidence and you stop enjoying it,' confessed Dave.

Altogether, including substitute roles, Dave made around 20 first-team appearances, netting his one and only senior goal in an FA Cup replay at non-league Runcorn. 'They had forced a draw at The Mem and an upset was on the cards. I came on with the side winning 2-1 and managed to make the game safe with the third goal,' he said with a smile.

In December 2003, and Rovers in turmoil, Dave left the club. 'My contract was up, there was a lot of cost cutting and I needed to get away,' admitted Dave.

An eight-month spell at Weston followed, the club gaining promotion to the Conference South, but it wasn't until Dave moved on to Southern Premier side Chippenham Town that he started to enjoy his football and to find the back of the net regularly.

Since then though, Dave has gone from strength to strength, moving on from Chippenham to Bath City and, more recently, Newport County. 'Former Rovers striker Steve White was originally the manager at Chippenham and it helped having a gaffer who knows what goal scoring is all about,' pointed out Dave. 'My goalscoring came back which boosts the confidence of any striker and I'm really enjoying life – my football and my job – now.'

Dave during his Rovers days.

Busy organising another hospitality event.

MIKE GREEN

Who captained the Rovers side that won promotion from the old Third Division in 1974 and, the following season, won promotion, again as captain, from the same division? The answer is Mike Green.

A solid, no-nonsense centre half, Mike began his career with Carlisle United. A former member of the Cumbria Schoolboys team, Mike was actually Carlisle's first apprentice.

'I remember making my debut at left back against Bristol City in April '65,' he recalled.

That season Carlisle went up as champions and Mike was to make a habit of promotion celebrations during his career. 'I had three years with Carlisle,' said Mike. 'Hughie McIlmoyle, who later had a spell with Bristol City, was the star player there.'

But, with first-team chances limited, Mike accepted a move to Gillingham in 1968. 'I started off in defence, but got moved up front and spent the best part of my three seasons there as a centre forward,' he revealed. 'We always seemed to be fighting against relegation, but I managed to score a few goals for them.'

Ironically, if it hadn't have been for a management change, Mike might never have come to Rovers in 1971. 'The manager told me I was being retained, then he got the sack and the chairman told me I wasn't.'

A few clubs were interested in signing Mike, but he chose to come to Rovers. 'Initially I struggled to break into the side as a striker, so persuaded Don Megson, who was in charge of the reserves, to play me at centre half and, after a few reserve games, got a place in the first-team defence.'

The switch proved a success for player and team and Watney Cup success was followed by promotion, with Mike missing just two games. He even had a stint in goal, taking over from an injured Jim Eadie in a match at Port Vale.

Having skippered the side to promotion and completed nearly 100 games for Rovers, it came as something of a shock to Mike when the manager told him they'd had an offer from Plymouth Argyle for him. 'I wasn't particularly keen,' admitted Mike. 'We'd just won promotion and had bought a house in Nailsea.'

But Mike went down to talk to Argyle and a deal was done. He was appointed skipper and, for the second successive year, led his team to promotion out of the Third Division.

'I liked Plymouth and thought I would finish my playing days there,' said Mike, who made over 100 starts for Argyle. 'We even bought a fish-and-chip shop in Cornwall. Then, out of the blue, I was offered the job of managing Torquay United.'

That was in 1977 and Mike combined playing and managing at Plainmoor. 'There were obvious difficulties in being player manager, but I enjoyed it,' said Mike. At one stage Mike was in a tug-of-war between Torquay and Rovers, who wanted him as their new manager. 'Rovers offered me the job, Torquay wanted compensation and I was piggie in the middle,' revealed Mike. The upshot was Mike stayed at Torquay, was given a new three-year contract, only to be sacked a year later.

For the next 22 years Mike ran a Post Office in Torquay, selling up five years ago – 'before Post Offices became an endangered species!'

Married to June, the couple live in Torquay and have a son (Christopher) and daughter (Zoe).

Rovers' promotion skipper Mike Green.

A round of golf for Mike these days.
(photo: Stuart MacDowell)

RON GREEN

You would think, by the end of their playing days, most footballers are pretty much travel sick. Journeys to places such as Walsall, West Bromwich, Shrewsbury, Scunthorpe, Manchester, Kidderminster, Colchester and Hereford must get a bit monotonous. And for Ron Green, that was just the home games! For the former Rovers goalkeeper had all those clubs on his cv at some stage of his career.

Ron began his league career with Walsall in 1977, notching up 160 league appearances in the first of three spells with the club. In the 1983/84 season Ron had a loan spell with West Brom, before moving on to Shrewsbury Town in the 84/85 pre-season. After 19 league appearances, though, Ron lost his place in the side and he came to Rovers.

'I went out to Rovers on loan, but before anything long term could be sorted out, David Williams left and Bobby Gould became boss,' he revealed.

But Ron's immediate future was not in doubt, with Gould quick to sign him to a permanent deal at Eastville. 'I lived in digs to start with and then we got a place in Clevedon – a lovely part of the world.'

Practically an ever present during his time with The Pirates, Ron settled down to life in the West Country, going on to make 56 appearances for Rovers. 'There were a good bunch of lads at the club, the fans were fantastic and everything was going well.' So it came as something as a shock to the keeper, when he picked up the paper to read that he was being transferred to Scunthorpe.

'It came out of the blue and I wasn't keen. We were happy where we were and, with my wife eight months pregnant, the last thing we wanted was another move.'

But with Rovers' cash flow problems making Ron's move a financial necessity, there was little choice and he was to spend two years between the sticks for 'Scunny', before being released in 1988. Like a lot of footballers, Ron was waiting for a call to get fixed up, but when it came, it wasn't from another Third or Fourth Division club, but from a top flight side – FA Cup winners Wimbledon, managed by his old Rovers' manager Bobby Gould.

'During my time with 'The Dons' I had half a dozen first-team games, but also went out on loan to Shrewsbury and then Manchester City,' revealed Ron.

Towards the end of the 88/89 season, Ron 'went home' – rejoining Walsall. 'It was nice to go back to the club and good for the family to return to their roots,' he pointed out.

After two more seasons with Walsall, Ron dropped down to play non-league with Alvechurch and Kidderminster Harriers, before returning to the Football League with Colchester. Ron played a handful of games for the Essex club, before trying his luck overseas in Hong Kong. 'To tell you the truth, I got homesick and came back after a month,' admitted Ron, who went on finish his career on the books of Cambridge United, Shrewsbury (yet again), Walsall (for a third time) and Hereford, signing non-contract forms to give the clubs goalkeeping cover.

Married to Maureen, the couple live in the Midlands and have two sons and a daughter. And like so many ex-pros, Ron is a postman.

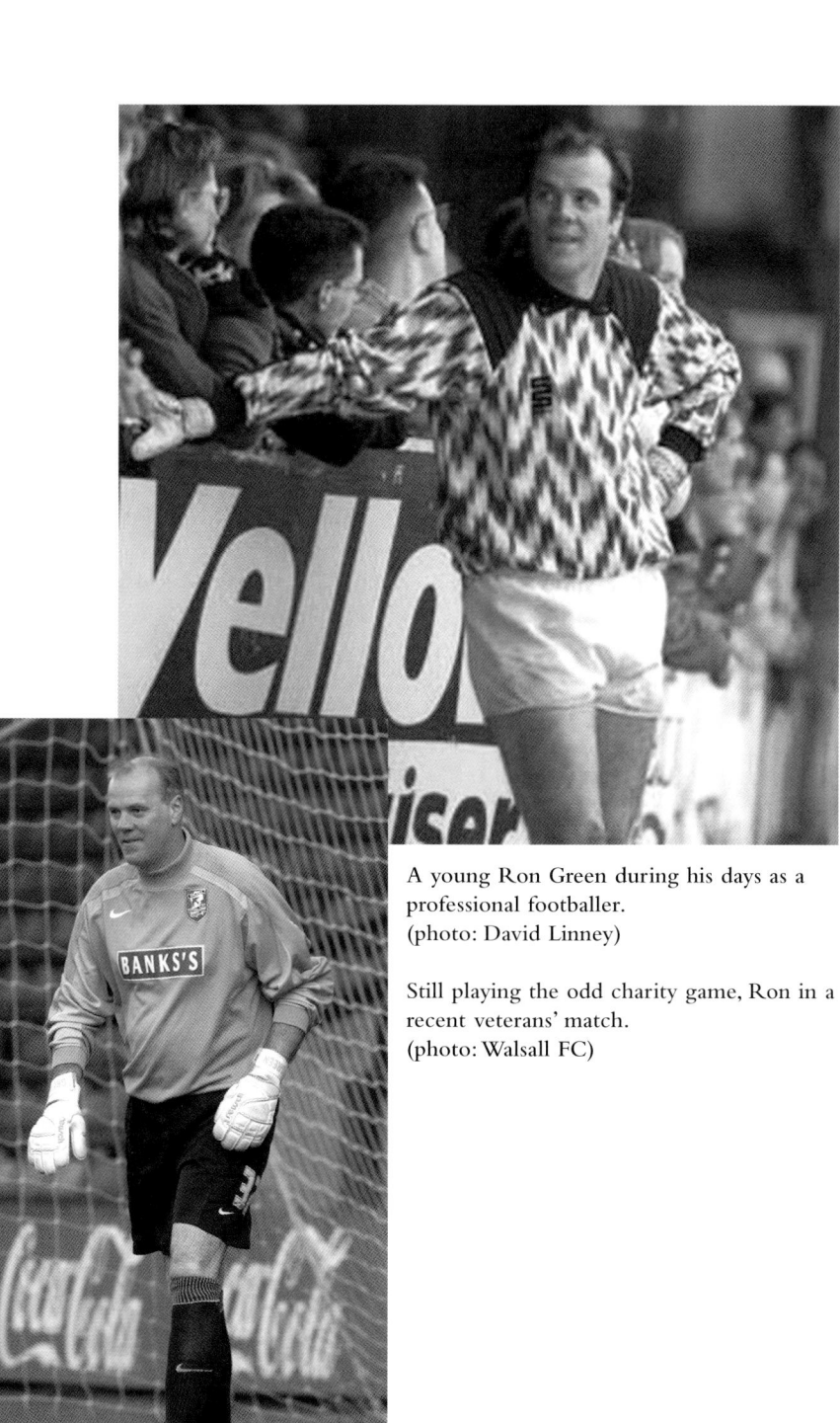

A young Ron Green during his days as a professional footballer.
(photo: David Linney)

Still playing the odd charity game, Ron in a recent veterans' match.
(photo: Walsall FC)

ANDY GURNEY

If you want to get on the right side of former Rovers defender Andy Gurney, don't mention the Play Offs. Four times he's been involved in Play Off matches and four times he's been a loser. 'That's three finals and one semi-final and we lost the lot,' said Andy. 'Just call me "lucky"!'

Andy joined Rovers as a YTS youngster in 1990. Signing pro forms in the summer of 1992, he made his league debut in the 93/94 season, the first of nearly 150 senior games for The Pirates.

'John Ward gave me my first start. An excellent manager who has always done well and I shall always be grateful to him,' said Andy. 'There was a great camaraderie in the squad and some very good players, like Marcus Stewart and Gareth Taylor, who both went on to bigger and better things,' he added.

The first Play Off disappointment for Andy came when Rovers lost out to Huddersfield Town in the Division Two Play Off Final at Wembley. 'It's every footballers dream to play at Wembley, which is quite different from Twerton Park!' said Andy. 'It was so disappointing to get that far and lose out.'

In the summer of 1997 Andy moved on to join Torquay United, under the management of Kevin Hodges. His all-action style and commitment to the cause helped his new side into the Play Offs, only for Andy to lose once more. But Andy's displays attracted the attention of higher league scouts and, after nearly switching to Wolves, Andy signed for Second Division Reading, with Torquay receiving a cheque for £100,000.

'Alan Pardew, another good manager, was in charge and the move went well,' said Andy. Over 70 appearances for 'The Royals' included more Play Off-heartache, before Andy moved to arch rivals Swindon Town.

In his first spell at the County Ground Andy made over 150 appearances and was given the captain's armband by manager Andy King. 'Andy did an excellent job at Swindon on a limited budget,' said Andy. The end of the 2003 season saw the club finish fifth, high enough for the Play Offs and a fourth dose of disappointment.

In 2004 Andy 'crossed the bridge' to sign for Swansea, where he was to enjoy a promotion season at last, but in the summer of 2005, a surprise move saw him rejoin Swindon, initially on loan.

'Up until then I had been lucky with injuries, but then I got an ankle injury at Huddersfield,' revealed Andy. 'I had an operation to take a piece of bone out, but the problem was still there.' Another op followed, but still the problem persisted. 'It got to the stage where I couldn't train properly and in the end I decided I'd have to quit full-time football.'

And so, after over 500 Football League games and more than 50 goals, Andy was forced to turn his back on the pro game. These days he works as a scaffolder and is player manager for local non-league side Weston-super-Mare.

Married to Clare, the couple have a young son and daughter and live in the Pilning area of Bristol.

Celebrating a goal for Rovers.

Andy today.

STEVE HARDING

Despite the fierce City-Rovers rivalry, many players make the transition from one side of Bristol to the other quite smoothly. One such former player is Steve Harding, a central defender who, before switching to the blue side of town, was a member of the 1976 Bristol City squad that won promotion to the top flight. Not that he got to play that many games in the City side that season – just two in fact. It wasn't until he moved to the north side of Bristol that he saw a fair bit more first-team action.

A former England Youth international, Steve came up through the ranks at Ashton. He was a member of the successful City youth side that got to the final of the FA Youth Cup in the 72/73 season, losing out over two legs to Ipswich Town, after overcoming the youth teams from some of the country's top sides, including Southampton, Arsenal and Everton.

After progressing to the reserves, Steve was faced with the problem of trying to claim a place in City's starting line-up. With City keeping a settled side, a move seemed the best solution. Initially Steve went out on loan to get first team football, with short-term moves to Southend United, Oxford United and Grimsby Town. And, in the summer of 1976, he made the transition from robin to pirate, signing for Rovers.

'I was desperate for first-team football and also was getting married that year, so it was important that my career progressed,' pointed out Steve. 'The funny thing was, Don Megson signed me and not long after that, left to work in The States.'

Steve made his Rovers debut in a 3-2 victory over Cardiff at Eastville, replacing Graham Day. He also got his name on the score sheet while with The Pirates, ensuring Rovers got a 1-1 draw at Luton in February '78. Over his four seasons with the club he made nearly 40 senior appearances, as well as playing four games for Brentford on loan. So, looking back, who was the toughest centre forward he had to face? 'Peter Withe, a real handful in his prime,' replied Steve. 'I was glad to see the back of him – in fact, whenever I had to mark him, I saw enough of his back as he went past me!

'I enjoyed my time at Rovers, but ultimately I fell out with Terry Cooper [manager at the time] and so it was time to move on,' said Steve philosophically.

After Rovers, Steve played in the local non-league circuit, first with Trowbridge Town, managed by former Chelsea star Alan Birchenal, then Gloucester City, Paulton Rovers and Mangotsfield.

Off the field Steve has had a varied career, working in school maintenance, later in a courier business and now with Mobile Windscreens, delivering to suppliers in an area that takes in Portsmouth, Southampton, Dorchester, Yeovil and the Midlands. 'I usually start around three in the morning, but am finished by mid-day,' said Steve, who lives in North Yate with his wife Michelle. The couple have a son and daughter.

'I enjoyed my time at both the Bristol clubs, although I notched up quite a few more games for Rovers.'

On the ball for Bristol Rovers.

Working with windscreens, Steve Harding today.

PAUL HARDYMAN

Today's footballers and managers often moan about not having sufficient breaks between games and sometimes having to play two, possibly three games in a week. Well, former Rovers full back Paul Hardyman, can put those whingers to shame, having played over 80 games in one season!

'It was actually eighty-four,' said Paul. 'I'd signed professional forms for 'Pompey' and was playing midweek games for their reserves and turning out regularly for non-league Waterlooville.'

Born in Portsmouth in 1964, Paul became an apprentice carpenter and joiner on leaving school, while playing football for Fareham Town and then Waterlooville. 'I had the choice of going to Villa, Brighton or Pompey,' revealed Paul. 'Signing for Portsmouth meant I could stay local and complete my carpentry apprenticeship.'

Paul made his first-team debut for 'Pompey' in March '84, coming on as a sub against Crystal Palace and his full debut a few weeks later. After over 150 games for Portsmouth, Paul moved on to Sunderland. 'My contract was up at Portsmouth and they offered me a one-year deal. I turned it down in favour of a three-year contract at Sunderland.'

Paul went on to enjoy a roller-coaster ride with 'The Black Cats'. 'I probably played the best football of my career there,' he said. 'I got nine goals in my first season and we went up to the (old) First Division, after Swindon were demoted, following financial irregularities.'

Paul's second season there saw the club relegated back to the (old) Second Division and his third year saw him in the Sunderland squad that got to play Liverpool in the FA Cup Final at Wembley. 'I started on the bench, which was a bit of a disappointment, as I'd played in every round up until then,' said Paul, adding that he did get on, albeit when the side were two goals down.

'After that I wanted to move back down south,' he revealed. 'Rovers came in for me, paying out £160,000, then a club record.'

It was a continuing case of 'never a dull moment' for Paul, who had no fewer than four managers in his first season with 'The Gas'. 'Denis Rofe signed me, then there was Malcolm Allison – a real character – then Steve Cross for a short time and finally John Ward, from who I learnt an awful lot.'

Living in Saltford, Paul enjoyed his time with Rovers, going on to play around 70 games for the Twerton Park-based side. 'Then I injured my knee and was out of the game for seven months,' said Paul. 'John Ward was very good and got me involved in scouting. There was also the possibility of a new contract, but the side lost in the Play Off Final at Wembley and that meant financial cutbacks and I was released.'

After Rovers, Paul had a year with Wycombe Wanderers and a spell with Barnet, before playing non-league with Slough and setting up his own carpentry business. Then he got the call to return to his roots at Portsmouth. 'Initially I was working with the club's football-in-the-community project and then got promoted to head coach at their Centre of Excellence,' he explained.

Married to Hazel, the couple have two sons, Robert and Mark, and live in Bournemouth.

Paul, during his time at Rovers.

Head coach of Portsmouth's Centre of Excellence, Paul Hardyman today. (photo: *The News*, Portsmouth)

PETER HIGGINS

The most popular profession entered into by former football pros in the Bristol area is that of postman. In fact, you could almost put out a full team of footballers-turned-posties. So it comes as no surprise to find that former Rovers winger Peter Higgins has also made the switch to Royal Mail.

'I've "been on the post" for over three years now,' said Peter. 'What I like best about the job is being out in the fresh air and having afternoons free at home, although the job is a lot harder than many people realize.'

Not that Peter began life in 'Civvy Street' as a postman. 'When I left full-time football I worked in the printing trade as a sales executive for twenty-five years,' he pointed out.

Peter's footballing life began when he signed for Bristol Rovers as a youngster in the sixties. 'Rovers had an excellent scouting system under Len Williams in Wales,' said the Cardiff-born winger. 'In fact, at Rovers training sessions we used to have England versus Wales practice matches. A lot of excellent Welsh talent went to Bristol Rovers – the best of them was probably Wayne Jones. It was a tragedy that injury curtailed his playing career so early, as he was a very talented player and one of the nicest men I've met in football.'

Between 1968 and 1973 Peter made around 50 appearances for The Pirates, scoring half a dozen goals. He played under Bert Tann, Fred Ford, Bill Dodgin and Don Megson during that time. He made his Rovers debut in March '69, a home defeat to Walsall, and went on to appear for the side in five consecutive seasons. His final match in Rovers' colours was in March '73, when they beat Rotherham three-nil at Eastville, with Peter scoring one of the goals and taking the Man of the Match award.

After leaving Bristol, Peter moved on to Doncaster Rovers, where he was to spend three years. The management team of former Manchester United defender Maurice Setters and his assistant, the late Johnny Quigley (a former Bristol City favourite), had assembled a young and talented side at Belle Vue. 'I was twenty-three when I joined them – and I was probably the oldest player on the books,' laughed Peter. 'They had some great young players, many of whom, like Terry Curran and Brendan Callaghan, went on to bigger clubs.'

After three years and over 70 games (plus a short loan spell at Torquay) Peter reluctantly bade farewell to the Yorkshire club. 'I loved my time there, I thought it was a smashing place,' he said.

Returning to his South-West roots, Peter signed as a part-timer with Bath City. 'One of my old team mates, Brian Godfrey, was manager and he built up a pretty useful side. In fact, I would say that Brian was the best manager I ever played for.'

After Bath City, Peter played for Cheltenham and Taunton, before helping Forest Green Rovers win the FA Vase in 1982. A broken leg two years later brought an end to his playing days, although he had spells as assistant manager at Forest Green, manager at Thornbury and coach at both Weston and Trowbridge.

Married to Julie and living in Kingswood, the couple both have three children from their previous marriages.

Peter in action for Rovers.

Peter Higgins today.

DAVID HILLIER

From footballer to fireman, that was the career path chosen by former Arsenal and Bristol Rovers midfielder David Hillier. 'It's something that appealed to me for some time,' said David. 'It's certainly a very worthwhile job and there are quite a few comparisons with life as a footballer, like the camaraderie and team work, for example.'

Not that it's a job that you can 'just walk into'. 'I had to go through three interviews before I was accepted in 2004 and am still having development training,' he revealed.

David was born in Blackheath, London on 19 December 1969, a good omen for a future footballer as it was also the day that Pele scored his one thousandth goal. He (David, not Pele!) joined Arsenal as an associate schoolboy in 1984, turning professional in 1988. He went on to captain the side that won the FA Youth Cup that same year and made his senior debut in a cup tie with Chester City two years later. That same season he made 16 appearances in Arsenal's title-winning team and went on to be selected for the England Under-21s side. In the 1992/93 campaign he made 43 appearances, but despite playing in two semi-finals – the Football League Cup and the FA Cup – he missed out on both finals owing to injury. 'That was a real choker,' he admitted.

The following year another injury forced him to miss playing in Arsenal's Cup Winners Cup Final success over Parma and although he featured in 'The Gunners' 2-1 defeat in the Cup Winners Final in 1995, he was sold to Portsmouth for £250,000, after 142 games for the north London side. After two-and-half years and 61 games for 'Pompey', he left to join up with 'Ollie's Army' at Bristol Rovers.

David made his Rovers debut in a 1-0 away defeat at Lincoln shortly after signing for The Pirates in February 1999. He went on to play 83 games for them, and even captained the side on one occasion. 'I enjoyed it at Rovers,' he said. 'The fans took to me, which is always a plus.' His one goal for Rovers came against Luton Town, in a 3-2 home win in August 2001. But injuries continued to get in the way, as David had tendonitis, then a neck injury, a knee operation and a broken toe, all in less than a year.

'Injuries certainly didn't help during my time at Rovers and there were the club's recurring financial problems, but for me, the club just wasn't the same when Ollie left – I thought he was a great manager.'

In March 2002, David played his last game for Rovers, a home defeat to Rushden & Diamonds, and the following summer signed for Barnet, before leaving professional football the following year.

Now living in the Emerson's Green area of Bristol, David is married to Zoë and they have two youngsters – Amy and Harry.

'What I liked about Rovers when I joined them was that, under Ollie, when they hit form they were on fire – which is a bit ironic now that I'm a fire fighter!' said David with a smile.

A pre-match photo of David the footballer.

Ready to answer the call as a fire fighter.

SCOTT HOWIE

There's a pub on the tip of Land's End with the self-explanatory name of 'The First and Last.' Or is it 'The Last and First'? Either way, former Rovers goalkeeper Scott Howie can lay claim to qualifying for his own 'last and first', having played in the last league game at Reading's old ground, Elm Park, and then in their first match at the superb Madejski Stadium.

'The last game at Elm Park was against one of my former clubs, Norwich,' recalled Scott, 'and the first at The Madejski at the start of the season was versus Luton – and I played in both matches.'

Prior to joining the elite group of Reading players to play on those two memorable occasions, Scott had started off his professional football career in the Scottish League with Clyde, where he had two seasons and was capped for Scotland Under-21s.

After around 70 appearances for Clyde, Scott was transferred, in 1993, to Norwich City for around £300,000. 'The Norwich manager was Mike Walker, a former goalkeeper, and his regular keeper was Bryan Gunn – an outstanding goalie. I was still learning the game and knew they could only make me a better goalkeeper.'

And so Scott continued to learn his trade, but Gunn's consistency meant Scott made just two league appearances. So, in 1994, he returned to his native Scotland, signing for Motherwell, where he made 137 appearances.

It was in 1998, after a short loan spell with Coventry, that Scott moved to Reading. 'They signed me on transfer deadline day, but the club was struggling and subsequently relegated, which, as it was their last season at Elm Park, was not the best way to finish a long association with the ground they'd played on for so many years.'

Scott went on to notch up around 100 games for 'The Royals', before joining Rovers in the summer of 2001. 'I was a regular in the side and got on really well with the manager, Gerry Francis,' recalled Scott. 'He could still play a bit and what he didn't know about football wasn't worth knowing.

'There were some good players at the club and the one that stood out was Latvian international Vitalijs Astafjevs – he was pure class.'

Again, Scott was nudging the 100-appearances figure when Rovers decided to let him go. 'Ray Graydon had taken over and wanted to build his own team,' explained Scott. 'He released a lot of the players he'd inherited, me included, but that's football.'

Although Scott's next club, Shrewsbury Town, dropped down into the Conference after his first season, he was to play a major role in helping them regain League status, saving three penalties in their 2004 Conference Play Off Final success.

Having moved home to Norwich, Scott left Shrewsbury for a season with Conference side Cambridge United, before deciding to hang up his boots and concentrate on his new career as a tax consultant. 'Knowing that football wasn't going to last forever, I had taken a course in business studies when I was younger,' revealed Scott. Having got his degree in the subject, Scott set up a tax consultancy business, specializing in advising sports people.

But the lure of playing is strong and when Scott was approached by non-league Kings Lynn, he was persuaded to don the green jersey again.

Married to Korinna, the couple have a young son, Solway.

An earlier playing days photograph of Scott.

Still shot stopping, a recent picture of tax consultant and Kings Lynn goalkeeper Scott Howie.
(photo: www.thisisthewalks.co.uk)

GRAHAM HYDE

There can't be many players who have played for their club side at Wembley four times in the space of just six weeks. Former Pirate Graham Hyde did, during his days as a player for Sheffield Wednesday.

'We got to the finals of both the League Cup and the FA Cup in 1993,' explained Graham. 'Because we had been drawn against local rivals Sheffield United in the semi-finals, the match was played at Wembley,' he went on. 'After beating United we returned to play Arsenal in the final. After drawing 1-1 with The Gunners, we lost the replay, again at Wembley, 2-1.'

OK, well that's three Wembley games, but what about the fourth? 'That was the League Cup Final, again at Wembley, and again versus Arsenal…and we lost that one,' he answered.

Graham had joined Wednesday as an apprentice in the late eighties. 'Howard Wilkinson was my first manager and one of my duties was to take him his tea,' said Graham. 'At that age you were always in awe of the boss but, despite what some people have said about him over the years, I got on fine with him and had a lot of respect for him.'

In September '91 Graham made his first-team debut in an away game with Manchester City. 'They had Peter Reid and Gary Megson in midfield, but we did OK, getting a 1-0 win,' said Graham. 'I enjoyed the occasion, but playing to a packed house at Maine Road was a lot different from playing in the youth or reserve sides.'

Graham was to enjoy 11 years and nearly 200 games at Hillsborough, before linking up with one of his former Wednesday managers, Trevor Francis, at Birmingham City. 'I had three years at Birmingham, but was unlucky with injuries,' pointed out Graham, who spent over four months on the sidelines with knee ligament problems. He had short loan spells at Chesterfield and Peterborough in order to regain match fitness, before signing for Rovers in November 2002.

Rovers were a struggling side at the time and manager Ray Graydon recognized that Graham's experience and combative midfield play were needed to turn things round. 'Rovers were fighting to avoid relegation to the bottom division and it was a difficult time, going right to the wire, with Rovers winning their last two games to stay up,' recalled Graham.

Having stayed up, Rovers started badly the following season, and Graydon, who had brought Graham to the club, paid for the bad results with his job. 'It was another season of struggle and upheaval,' said Graham, who went on to play over 60 games for The Pirates, before being released.

After Rovers, Graham had a season with Graham Turner's Hereford United, as they fought to regain their League status, moved on to Worcester City for three quarters of a season and then had a short spell with Hednesford Town. Later, Graham joined forces with former team mate Martin O'Connor as assistant manager and coach at Halesowen Town and, more recently, signed for Fleet Town, managed by another player he's lined up with before – Andy Sinton.

Married to Emma, the couple live in Solihull and have a young daughter (Olivia) and baby son (Callum).

'Looking back, I enjoyed playing for Rovers, but those Wembley appearances will always mean something extra special to me,' summed up Graham.

Graham in action for Wednesday.

A more recent photo of Graham.

WAYNE JONES

Wayne Jones, a talented inside forward, began his time with Rovers as a 14-year-old, playing in the youth and A teams. He signed professional forms in 1966, making his league debut in February 1967 in a home win over Doncaster Rovers. Born in Treorchy, he gained amateur youth caps for Wales, went on to win eight Under-23 caps and later broke into the full international side.

'I have some great memories from my playing days,' said Wayne. 'When I gained my first Under-23 cap, Rovers manager Bert Tann arranged for all my team mates to go to Swansea to cheer me on. A few years later I played against an England Under-23s side that included my old team mate Larry Lloyd, by then making a name for himself with Liverpool.'

Other matches that stand out for Wayne, include cup successes over Bolton Wanderers and Manchester United, both away from home. 'In the Bolton match I started as sub, but came on when Lindsay Parsons got injured,' recalled Wayne. 'We were one-nil down when I managed to score two crackers, one with either foot, and we won 2-1.'

And the Old Trafford game? 'A great night for Rovers,' he replied with a smile. 'They had drawn at Eastville, but we went up there playing against a forward line of Morgan, Kidd, Charlton, Best and Storey-Moore and won 2-1. Fantastic.'

Having helped Rovers win the Watney Cup and made his full international debut for Wales – a 1-nil win over Finland – things were looking good for the young Welshman. He had notched up well over 250 games for Rovers, scoring 36 goals. But in November '72, a very promising future was snatched away from him, as he crumbled to the Eastville turf, with no opposing players within yards of him. 'Cartilege trouble was suspected to begin with, but after I'd had an exploratory operation, the surgeon told me I had the knee of a seventy-year-old, riddled with arthritis and if I attempted to carry on playing I would become a cripple,' revealed Wayne.

So, at the age of 24, and having already been selected for his second Welsh cap, Wayne had to reluctantly look for a new career. 'Rovers were very good to me and, after I'd decided that I wanted to get into the medical side of football, treating injuries, they gave me the opportunity to do just that,' he said.

Having obtained the necessary qualifications, Wayne left Rovers and accepted an invitation from Graham Turner to be a coach/physio at Shrewsbury. He was to link back up with Graham later in his career, but after three years there, he couldn't resist a return to Eastville as assistant manager to David Williams. 'David is a good friend, but when he left Rovers and Bobby Gould came, I moved on and had a year as physio and coach to Rayyan in the United Arab Emirates, a fantastic experience.'

On returning to the UK, Wayne had two spells with Notts County, the latter including a time as acting manager, Huddersfield Town (three years as physio), ten years at Gillingham and Hereford United. Until recent times he was the physio at Yeovil Town.

Married to Kay, the couple have a son and daughter, while Wayne has two daughters from his previous marriage.

Wayne in action for Rovers.

Wayne Jones today.

GAVIN KELLY

If you ever go out for 'a Chinese' with former Rovers goalkeeper Gavin Kelly, the chances are chicken curry will not be his first choice. 'I was playing in Hong Kong and went to a Chinese restaurant. I ordered the chicken curry and it came complete with the head! Put me right off chicken curry for life!'

Long before Gavin was having nightmares about Chinese cuisine, he was looking to curry favour (sorry!) as a Football League shot stopper. 'I'd played schoolboy, county and local league football as a youngster in East Riding, before being becoming an apprentice with Hull City,' he said.

Signing full-time in 1987, he made his senior debut the following year. After a dozen or so games for 'The Tigers', Gavin accepted a move to Rovers. 'Gerry Francis signed me, initially as cover for Brian Parkin, on transfer deadline day 1989.'

Originally living in Mangotsfield and later Keynsham, Gavin has fond memories of his time with Rovers. 'There were some fantastic games, not least was beating Bristol City at Twerton and winning the Third Division championship,' he said. 'The game at Wembley against Tranmere in the Leyland Daf Cup was also special.'

Gavin also has fond memories of other cup games with Rovers. 'We'd drawn Aston Villa at home and there was no love lost between the two managers at the time – Ron Atkinson and Malcolm Allison. We were one down when Villa got a penalty. Dean Saunders took it but I managed to save it and we went on to earn a replay.'

Villa won the replay but, proving that lightning can strike twice, Kelly again denied them a goal from the spot. 'We were losing one-nil, when Villa were given another penalty. This time Ray Houghton took it and again I managed to keep it out.'

Gavin laughs at the way modern footballers are treated today. 'They don't know they're born. Luxury dressing rooms... top class training facilities... special diets. We used to train at a chocolate factory with portakabins for changing, play at a cramped non-league ground and as far as diets were concerned, we would stop the coach on the way back from away games for fish and chips.'

Towards the end of his time at Rovers, John Ward had taken over the manager's chair and Gavin was a frequent visitor to his office. 'I was pestering John because I desperately wanted first-team football. The trouble was that Brian Parkin was on top form and I couldn't really complain about not playing.'

And so, after 30 league games for The Pirates, Gavin decided it was time to try his luck elsewhere and he signed for Scarborough, a league club at that time. 'On paper it was ideal – just twenty miles from my old home, but it wasn't a good move.'

A year in Hong Kong followed his two seasons with Scarborough. 'It was a brilliant experience, but it was so hot that in one game I thought I was going to pass out.'

After returning from China, Gavin went on to play non-league football with North Ferriby United, Whitby Town and Bradford Park Avenue. He even returned to Scarborough as player-coach, before finishing his playing days with Unibond League side Bridlington Town.

A shift worker for a malt products company, Gavin also runs his own soccer school. He lives in Bridlington with partner Julie – miles from the nearest Chinese takeaway!

Gavin in his Rovers days.

Gavin Kelly today.
(photo: Dominick Taylor)

LARRY LLOYD

When you think about it, there aren't many 'hard men' left in football. Years ago every team had one. And they had great nicknames, like 'Razor', 'Chopper' and 'Iron Man'. At Ashton Gate, Norman 'Bites Yer Legs' Hunter was a hard case and, from the blue side of town, there was Larry Lloyd – a player you definitely didn't take liberties with.

So, where do you start with Larry? He played with the best and for the best and won just about every major honour going. Not bad for someone from a north Bristol council estate, one of ten children.

At the age of 14 Larry signed for Rovers – their first ever associate schoolboy. When he left school he desperately wanted to go full time and become an apprentice. But, with money tight, he had to get 'a proper job'. 'I had eighteen months working for an engineering company and hated it.'

Larry was still working at his day job and training as an amateur at Rovers in the evening, when he was called up for his senior debut – against Bristol City in the annual end-of-season event, the Gloucestershire Cup Final. Although Rovers lost 3-1, Larry did well and it must have seemed that all his Christmases had come at once when he was offered a full time contract.

'I reported for pre-season training in the summer of 67, a local lad playing for the team I'd adored since I was eight, and here I was alongside Alfie Biggs, Harold Jarman, Dougie Hillard and Ray Mabbutt – heroes that I used to queue up to get autographs from.'

But Larry had to be patient. 'I didn't get a sniff of first-team action in that first season,' recalled Larry. 'Stuart Taylor was the regular centre half and he was very consistent and never got injured or suspended.' But when Fred Ford took over team selection, Larry got his chance. 'Fred decided to play both myself and Stuart as central defenders and, although we weren't doing well in the league, we went on a good cup run, which culminated in a narrow defeat at Everton.'

Watching that game was Liverpool manager Bill Shankly. A close friend of Fred Ford, 'Shanks' had been having Larry watched and so, after just 51 games for Rovers, Larry went to Anfield for a fee of £55,000.

From that time until he hung up his boots, it was success after success for the determined Bristolian. FA Cup Finals, League championship, UEFA Cup winner… it goes on and on. A move to Coventry City in 1974 was, on his own admission, a bad move, but there were still the glory days at Forest to come, with promotion, the League championship and two European Cup Final wins. And let's not forget his England international appearances, four in England Youths, eight in the Under-23s side, which he went on to skipper, and four full England caps.

Later, Larry enjoyed success as player-manager at Wigan, and also had a spell as Notts County's boss.

Since leaving the game, Larry has been a publican, worked as a PR manager for Forest and been a soccer commentator on local radio, before emigrating to Spain, where he ran a bar (Lloyd No 5) in the resort of Fuengirola.

These days he's still in Spain, where he's a property salesman. He has a daughter and son from his first marriage and also a granddaughter.

Larry (right) in action for Forest against Rovers at Eastville.

Larry Lloyd and his aptly named autobiography – *Hard Man: Hard Game.*

LEE MADDISON

All the former Pirates players featured in this book have had their ups and downs. But they pale somewhat when compared to former Rovers full back Lee Maddison, who owes his life to his brother, who donated bone marrow in order for Lee to survive serious illness.

'In 2004 I was diagnosed with non-Hodgkin's lymphoma – a rare form of leukemia,' said Lee. 'I was very ill and football took very much a back seat. I had three months of intensive chemotherapy and radio treatment and was receiving blood transfusions daily.'

Now we all know that it doesn't matter who or what you are, there are illnesses that are quite indiscriminate when it comes to who they attack. Fortunately Lee was lucky. Brother Neil's bone marrow was a perfect match and Lee came through the blackest period in his life.

When Lee started off pursuing a career as a footballer, he couldn't possibly have foreseen how things were to turn out. 'Gerry Francis was my first manager and he was very good and very tactically aware,' said Lee. He made his senior debut at left back in the 1991/92 season, in a cup game against Plymouth and his league debut the following week in a home game with Tranmere.

Between 1991 and 1995, Lee was to make 73 league appearances for The Pirates, playing under Francis, Martin Dobson, Dennis Rofe, Malcolm Allison and John Ward. He also had a loan spell with Bath City. But, in September '95, anxious for first-team football, Lee signed for Northampton Town. 'Ian Atkins was manager there at the time and he later went on to sign me at two more clubs, so he must have rated me.'

After two seasons with 'The Cobblers', Lee tried his luck north of the border with Dundee. 'I had four seasons up there and loved it,' he recalled. 'We won promotion in my first season and it was a brilliant to play at the likes of Rangers and Celtic.'

Reunited with Atkins at Carlisle in October 2000, Lee had four years with the club and was a sub in the LDV Vans Trophy Final against Bristol City at The Millenium Stadium in 2003. 'I came on for the last twenty-five minutes and although we lost (2-0) it was a great experience.'

During his time with Carlisle, Lee went out on loan to Oxford, where he again played for Atkins.

Lee's last season at Carlisle ended with relegation and he went back to Scotland, joining Scottish league new boys Gretna. 'I had three seasons there, but all that ground to a halt when I was diagnosed with leukaemia.'

After his successful battle with the illness, Lee joined the club's coaching staff, but after the club ran into financial difficulties he lost his job.

Disillusioned with the game, Lee made a fresh start, moving down to Hampshire with his wife Angela and their two young daughters, Holly and Jazmine. Like so many other former Bristol footballers, Lee opted for the outdoor life as a postie and also runs local soccer schools for youngsters.

He has never forgotten how much he owes to the health service and regularly promotes the blood transfusion service, taking part in fund-raising activities. 'After what I went through, you tend to look at life differently,' summed up Lee.

Lee in his playing days with
Northampton Town.
(photo: Peter Norton Photography of
Northampton)

Back in Bristol, Lee Maddison today.

RONNIE MAUGE

If you asked the supporters of clubs such as Bury and, nearer home, Plymouth Argyle or Bristol Rovers, what the C stands for in Ronnie C Mauge, the answer could well be 'Commitment'. 'I may not have been the game's most technically gifted player, but as soon as I got on the pitch, I always gave everything, one hundred and ten per cent,' said Ronnie.

Ronnie's professional career began when he joined Charlton Athletic as a trainee. After failing to break into the first team, he moved on to Third Division Fulham, where, over two seasons, he made around 60 senior appearances. His all-action midfield displays attracted the attention of Bury and a £40,000 transfer fee saw him join them in 1990.

'It was while I was at Bury that the possibility of a move to Manchester City came about,' revealed Ronnie. 'I went to Maine Road on loan, but got injured, having made just one sub appearance and the deal fell through.'

After well over 100 games for Bury, Ronnie moved to the South West, joining Neil Warnock's Plymouth Argyle in another £40,000 transfer. 'I love and adore that man,' said Ronnie. 'He was a big influence on my career and on my life.'

Describing his time at Argyle as a 'roller-coaster ride on and off the pitch,' Ronnie quickly won over the fans with his whole-hearted efforts. And that adulation was repaid when he became the first ever Argyle player to score a goal at Wembley, as 'The Pilgrims' beat Darlington one-nil to win the 1996 Third Division promotion Play Off Final.

'Plymouth will always have a place in my heart,' said Ronnie. 'I had some great years there, got to know some wonderful people and it's where I met my wife Tracey and where the first of our two sons was born.' But, after four years and nearly 150 games at Argyle, he moved on to join Rovers, managed by Ian Holloway.

'Without doubt, Ollie is the best I've ever played for,' Ronnie told me. 'It was a privilege to play for the man – I still ring him for advice to this day.'

But a Rovers team that seemed promotion certainties for much of the season, suddenly 'blew up' and missed out on even making the Play Offs. 'We were going really well and then suddenly nose dived and finished seventh,' recalled Ronnie.

As is often the way in football, the manager carried the can and Ollie was sacked. 'That was the worse decision Rovers ever made – he was the heartbeat of the club.'

Ronnie was to stay at Rovers until 2001, winning the last of his eight caps for the Trinidad & Tobago national team while a 'Gashead'. But it was while he was in the national side that Ronnie suffered a broken leg, an injury that was to ultimately spell the end of his professional career, though he did battle back and made a few more appearances (Ronnie made over 60 in total for Rovers) before calling it a day.

'After that we moved to Ipswich, and I had a spell as manager of Whitton United in the Eastern Counties League.'

A football development officer for Ipswich Borough Council and a director of the Kieron Dyer School of Soccer, Ronnie added; 'As a football manager, one thing I soon realized was just how difficult I must have been as a player!'

Ronnie the Rover.

Ronnie the football manager.

CHRISTIAN McCLEAN

A late starter in the pro game, versatile Christian McClean is quite a diverse sort of a guy. He's not averse to a bit of classical music; was nicknamed 'The Beast' by Rovers fans, yet went on to help others in the community – first working in a care home and now with the London Fire Brigade.

Born in Colchester, Christian joined his home town club, going on to play in their youth and reserve sides. 'I never actually signed full-time forms and left to play for Zeeburgia in Amsterdam,' said Christian.

Returning to England in 1984, Christian played non-league football while working as a rep for a record company specializing in classical music. But he had not given up on soccer, writing off to a number of clubs for a trial.

'I was invited down to Rovers and played in some reserve matches and also the old Gloucester Cup Final against City,' revealed Christian. 'After that I was initially signed up for the rest of the season.'

Equally at home at centre half or centre forward, Christian made his debut in a one-nil win at Chesterfield and was in the side that faced Bury at Twerton Park three days later.

'Two games in three days was very tiring,' admitted Christian. 'I was twenty-four and had only been in full-time training a week or so.'

In Christian's first full season at Rovers – 1988/89 – he made 28 senior league appearances, with the club just losing out in the Play Offs. The following year they were back with a bang, winning the Third Division championship and just losing out to Tranmere Rovers in the Leyland Daf Final at Wembley. Christian scored in three consecutive games to help his side win crucial games and he also came on as a sub at Wembley.

Promoted to the old Second Division, Christian was forced to miss much of the season thanks to a hip problem that required surgery. 'At the end of the season I was offered a new contract but with Gerry (Francis) off to QPR and my having missed so many games, I asked to released.'

A move to Swansea seemed to be the new start that Christian was looking for. 'The problem was I was desperate to get fit and rushed back too soon,' he admitted. 'I did get to play against Monaco in the European Cup Winners Cup at Swansea, but missed the return leg.'

Christian left 'The Swans' after just a handful of games and headed home to Colchester. 'Then I got a call from Northampton manager Theo Foley, asking me to join them.'

With Northampton struggling financially, Christian had to make do with being a non-contract player. But he did go on to play a couple of dozen games, before finding himself out of work again. 'The club was broke and the creditors were called in. I was one of ten players released, along with the manager.'

Spells in non-league football followed, while off the pitch Christian decided it was time to start a new career and got a job in the care industry, going on to become manager of a care home. Later, he changed tack by joining the London Fire Service.

'Looking back, I was very lucky. I came into football late and ended up with two medals in only my second full season – there are plenty of pros who've played for years and don't even have one medal to show for it.'

Christian in his Rovers days.

Ready for an emergency, fireman Christian McClean today.

JEFF MEACHAM

The majority of former Rovers players in this book have long since hung up their boots. But not striker Jeff Meacham. His motto is 'have boots will travel' – and he is still playing local non-league soccer today, despite being in his mid-forties. 'As long as I can keep myself fit and don't lose the desire to get out on the pitch, then I'll keep on playing, but only when needed,' said Jeff.

A familiar face in the local non-league scene, Jeff has worn the colours of Almondsbury Greenway, Longwell Green, Forest Green Rovers, Bath City, Trowbridge, Patchway and Gloucester City – to name but a few! In fact, he'd been to so many clubs that he seemed to start all over again and had second sessions with at least three of them!

It was while Jeff was playing at Trowbridge that he caught the eye of the Bristol Rovers scouts. 'That was in '86 and Bobby Gould was manager of Rovers,' recalled Jeff. Making the step up from non-league to professional football is tough enough for most, but Jeff did it the hard way, signing part-time for Rovers and keeping 'the day job'.

'I was – still am – a cable joiner with SWEB, now Western Power, and although I was going to give my chance with Rovers my best shot, I didn't want to lose the security of "a proper job". You could say I was combining electricity with gas!'

Despite training away from the squad in the evenings, Jeff made good progress, scoring on his debut for Rovers reserves. After a while Jeff was told he would be travelling with the first team to Chesterfield to gain experience. 'I was under the impression that I was just going along for the ride, but when we got to the ground, Bobby told me I was playing. That was typical Bobby Gould,' he said.

After Bobby left for Wimbledon, Jeff found himself playing for one of his boyhood heroes – Gerry Francis. 'As a kid I used to support QPR and Gerry was my idol,' reminisced Jeff.

Over the next two seasons Jeff went on to make close on 50 appearances in all competitions, netting around a dozen goals, although his nine League goals were all scored at Twerton Park. But with Devon White and Gary Penrice established as first choice strikers, Jeff decided it was time to move on. 'All I've ever wanted to do was to play football and with Rovers having no reserve side I couldn't get a game,' he added. 'There were no bad feelings, I just wanted to play.'

A move to Weymouth followed, but it never really worked out, so Jeff returned to one of his former clubs, Bath City, before moving on to play for a number of local non-league clubs.

These days Jeff has made the step up to player/manager, looking after Western League side Brislington. 'I'm enjoying the experience and, as manager, I can make sure I can get a game every week if I want to!'

Married to Helen, the couple live in Filton and have a teenage son (Ryan) and daughter (Bethany).

Jeff as a Bristol Rover.

Jeff at work for Western Power.

MICHAEL MEAKER

One man putting his years as a professional soccer player to good use is Michael 'Meaks' Meaker, who is now an agent. Not the 007 James Bond type of agent – not that the all action Mister Bond kicked anything but bad guys. 'I've been working as an agent for about two or three years now,' explained Michael. 'I'd always wanted to stay in the game and I actually left playing full-time to concentrate on qualifying as a football agent.'

During his career, Michael clocked up a total of 358 senior appearances for the clubs that he played for, including a three-year spell with Bristol Rovers. A talented winger, he also made nine appearances for the Wales Under-21 team, as well as playing alongside Ryan Giggs, Mark Hughes, Vinnie Jones and Neville Southall in the Welsh side.

Michael started with Queens Park Rangers on their youth training scheme in 1990, going on to make his league debut in December that year, when he came on as a substitute in an away game with Manchester City. He went on to make close on 100 appearances during his five years at Loftus Road, as well as enjoying a short but successful loan spell with Plymouth Argyle.

'Gerry Francis did a superb job at Rangers, taking the club to fifth place in the Premiership,' stated Michael. 'He was an outstanding manager who could bring the best out of his players.'

In the summer of 1995 Michael, who also enjoyed a loan spell with Sheffield United, was transferred to Reading for over £550,000. He played close on 100 games for 'The Royals', before joining Rovers at the start of the 1998/99 season. He made a dream start, scoring on his debut against his former club Reading.

'Ollie [Ian Holloway] and Penny [Gary Penrice] brought me to Rovers,' recalled Michael. 'They had some very good players, such as Jamie Cureton, Nathan Ellington and Jason Roberts. There was also Andy Tillson, who I knew from my time at QPR. An excellent pro and a really nice bloke.'

Injuries to his shoulder and back restricted Michael, who also had loan spells at Swindon and Chesterfield, to around 30 games in Rovers colours. 'I thoroughly enjoyed my time with Rovers, but they were having some financial difficulties, so I moved on in 2001, returning to play for Plymouth.'

Michael was to play a dozen or so games for Argyle, but decided Plymouth wasn't for him. 'Argyle is a great club and I got on fine with my team mates and the manager, but I simply couldn't settle there,' he explained.

Michael moved into non-league soccer, playing for Northwich Victoria, Henley Town and Southall, before returning to the region to play for Mangotsfield, helping them to win the Southern League (Western Division) championship in 2005. Hounslow Borough was the next side to benefit from his services, before another spell at Mangotsfield. These days he plays and coaches in the Western League with Bitton. He and his business partner Steve Porter also run a football academy in Bristol.

'I've had five agents during my career and learnt a lot from all of them,' said Michael. 'It's a funny business to be in and you are often burning the midnight oil, especially when the transfer windows are in place, but I am enjoying the challenge.'

Michael Meaker on the ball for Rovers.

A busy life as a football agent for Michael today.

DON MEGSON

In 1966 history was made at Wembley, when Sheffield Wednesday's Don Megson became the first captain to lead his side on a lap of honour after LOSING in the FA Cup Final. 'Normally the beaten team just collected their losers' medals and slunk away, but we'd contributed to an excellent final and I felt it was the right thing to do,' explained Don, who went on to join Rovers as player/coach and later manager.

A Sheffield Wednesday legend, Don made 442 appearances for the club over an 18 year period. He made his league debut in the late fifties and when he got into the side, they went on an unbeaten run of 19 games. 'I don't pretend to take all the credit for that, but that's how your luck goes sometimes.' And Don was also lucky when it came to injuries. 'I think I only missed a dozen games in eleven years,' he mused.

In March 1970, Don decided to take up a new challenge when offered a role as player-coach with Rovers. 'After so many years with Wednesday it was a wrench to leave, but the prospect of getting on the coaching ladder appealed to me.'

Don was to spend eight years with Rovers and loved practically every minute. 'Bert Tann had moved 'upstairs' as general manager and I worked as assistant to Bill Dodgin and alongside Bobby Campbell. I learnt a great deal from them.'

In a natural progression, Don, who played 31 games for The Pirates, took over the management reins from Dodgin and in only his third game in charge, led the team to their first national trophy success, when they won The Watney Cup.

'We had a good side and, in 1973/74, deservedly won promotion to the old Second Division,' continued Don. Ah, the promotion year and that 8-2 win at Brighton. Did he share the traditional post-match drink with Cloughie afterwards? 'No, I didn't,' was Don's swift reply. 'I never got on with Brian Clough. The one thing that annoyed me about that game was that, while he publicly lambasted his side, he never once gave us any credit for a superb performance.'

Despite some very good offers to manage elsewhere, Don stuck with Rovers. But, as time went on, he became disillusioned. 'The club appeared to be standing still and we were looking at survival rather than progress. In fairness, gates not reaching expectations didn't help. When I was told that I'd have to sell our better players, the writing was on the wall.'

Having previously turned down overtures from other clubs, in 1977 Don finally succumbed, accepting a three-year contract to manage Portland Timbers in the North American Football League. 'I loved it over there, it was an unbelievable lifestyle.'

After returning from The States, Don had a year managing Bournemouth and then scouted for a number of clubs, before retiring. Back home in Sheffield, he lives just five miles away from son Gary. His other son, Neil, still lives in America.

Don also has three grandchildren, Alex and Samantha in The States and Gary's lad, Simon, in Sheffield. Sadly, Don's wife Yvonne died four years ago. 'That was the worse time in my life,' said Don.

'I've always been the sort of person to put down roots,' summed up Don. 'I had a large slice of my life with Wednesday, eight years with Rovers and three in America – lots of very good memories.'

Player, coach and manager, Don Megson during his Rovers days.

Don Megson today.

KEVIN MILLER

Despite big money transfers and all the trappings that go with being a professional footballer, Falmouth-born Kevin Miller has never forgotten his roots. 'I've got a lot of friends in Devon and Cornwall and have kept in touch with them throughout my career. I've never lost sight of how lucky I was and how good football has been to me,' said the goalkeeper who has been the last line of defence for Exeter (twice), Birmingham, Watford, Crystal Palace, Barnsley, Bristol Rovers, Southampton and Torquay.

These days Kevin is now 'back home' living in Penryn, turning out for Bodmin Town and running football-in-the-community coaching sessions, with another ex pro, John Hodge.

Kevin's big chance came when he was spotted by Exeter City, playing in goal for Newquay. 'Terry Cooper signed me on non-contract terms, but then they had a goalkeeping crisis and I was in for the next three games,' he explained. It couldn't have gone better, with Kevin conceding just one goal. 'I signed full time and went on to play nearly two hundred games for the club, which included getting promotion from the old Fourth Division, which we won by ten points.' Kevin also picked up his first coveted Player of the Year Award.

Kevin's agility between the posts meant that he would be moving on. 'Terry Cooper had gone on to Birmingham City, a very big club, and he came back to Exeter to take me to St Andrews,' recalled Kevin, whose transfer brought in a much appreciated £250,000.

A change of manager and Kevin was on his way, this time to Watford, again for £250,000. 'Watford was a great move for me,' said Kevin, who played 148 senior games and won Player of the Year twice in his three years there. The summer of '97 saw him signing for Premiership club Crystal Palace, who paid Watford £1.5million for his services.

In August 1999 Kevin signed for Barnsley, spending three years at Oakwell, before returning to the South West and his first professional club Exeter. 'Unfortunately, the club had all sorts of problems and were relegated from the Football League. It was heart breaking.'

Despite Kevin undergoing knee surgery in the summer of 2003, Rovers manager Ray Graydon wasted no time in signing him. 'I was playing in goal sixteen days after surgery,' said Kevin. But, despite his best efforts in Rovers goal, the team struggled to get results. 'I always felt we had a decent side, but we under-achieved and subsequently struggled,' pointed out Kevin. With results continuing to go against them, manager Graydon was axed. 'Phil Bater took over, but was not really given enough time. Then came Ian Atkins…'

Kevin was to make nearly 80 appearances for The Pirates and also had three months on loan at Derby. 'After that I stopped playing, moved to London and worked in corporate hospitality,' said Kevin. But a surprise SOS from Southampton saw him back in action. 'They had a goalkeeping crisis and I played in their last eight league games, which, having walked away from the game, was a bonus.'

The last seven of Kevin's 700+ League games saw him between the posts at Torquay United. 'Not one of the highlights of my career,' admitted Kevin.

'Now, I've come back to my roots and through the football-in-the-community scheme, I can give something back, so I'm happy.'

Over 700 appearances as a pro, goalkeeper Kevin Miller.

Passing on the benefits of experience to the footballers of tomorrow, Kevin Miller today.
(photo: Terry Harry)

TREVOR MORGAN

So how many Rovers fans knew that much-travelled striker Trevor Morgan has the distinction of scoring their last league goal at Eastville and also their first league goal at Bath? Well he did. 'The goal at Eastville was a volley against Chesterfield and the one at Twerton was a penalty against Bolton,' he said.

Trevor, who had two spells with local rivals Bristol City and three at Exeter, joined The Pirates in September '85. 'I was at Exeter, but was not happy with my performance. The travelling from Clevedon was getting me down and, for the only time in my career, I asked for a transfer,' said Trevor. 'I was delighted when Rovers came in for me – for one thing, it meant we didn't have to move again.'

Understandably, Trevor, with his City background, had to win over the Rovers fans. 'I started off well, getting eight goals in five games, so I think any connection to City was quickly forgiven.'

Trevor was to play 55 league games, scoring 26 league goals for them, during his 16 months with the club. But, on New Year's Day 1987, Trevor was moving back across town for a second spell with City. 'Rovers were in a transitional period, moving on some of the senior players. Bobby Gould called me in to say City had made an offer for me and that was that.'

Prior to playing for the two Bristol sides, Trevor's league career began on the coast with Bournemouth. He had two spells with the club, with a move to Mansfield sandwiched in between, before joining City in March 1983. After City came his first spell at Exeter.

It was during his time with Exeter that Trevor had a second taste of Australian soccer (he'd actually had a spell in Melbourne before the start of his league career). 'I was a guest player for a team in Sydney. It was a wonderful experience.'

After returning to St James Park, Trevor played just a handful of games, before getting the call to join Rovers.

In June '87, Trevor moved again – this time to Fourth Division Bolton Wanderers. He helped the club gain promotion, before moving on to Colchester. Although the club had a disastrous season, resulting in relegation to the Conference, Trevor again made the record books, scoring their last league goal.

After Colchester, the Morgan family enjoyed three months in Hong Kong, Trevor playing for Happy Valley, before the chance to link up with Terry Cooper saw him return to Exeter as player coach. 'At the end of that season I went back to Hong Kong.'

Trevor returned to the UK to link up twice more with Cooper, as his assistant manager at first Birmingham and then Exeter.

After that Trevor headed back to the sunshine, destination Western Perth, coaching Sorrento FC. 'We won every major title there and, after two years, I was appointed the head coach of the West Australian Institute of Sport. Later I moved on to Singapore, becoming head coach of Sarawak.'

After leaving Sarawak, Trevor went back to Perth, but he has since returned to the UK, taking up a coaching position at Hull City last season.

Married to Jackie, the couple have three children, Lauren, James and Alex.

'Looking back on my days with Rovers, it's nice to think that, long after I've gone, those goals at Eastville and Twerton will probably feature in one of those soccer trivia quizzes!'

Trevor during his playing days in Bristol.

Time to relax in their back garden, Trevor and his wife Jackie.

PAUL NIXON

Born in County Durham, Paul Nixon was not unduly worried about how far he had to travel to play football. 'I bumped into a friend who was playing in New Zealand and mentioned that I'd be interested in giving it a go over there. I got a call shortly after and grabbed the first flight out.'

Paul was soon making his mark on the soccer field, bagging 80 goals for Claudeland Rovers in two seasons. Next was Gisborne City, where he helped the team to cup success and a runners-up spot in the National League. With the endorsement of a Kiwi passport, he also went on to gain six international caps.

During his first stint in New Zealand, Paul held a variety of jobs, including working in an old people's home, meat stacker, gardener and travelling salesman.

'I came home in '88 to introduce my future wife Wilma to my folks. We planned to stay for eight weeks, but it would be eight years before we got back to New Zealand.'

It was during his visit that a mutual love of pigeons saw Paul end up at Twerton Park. 'I was playing a few games for Seaham Red Star and the trainer asked if I was interested in playing pro football in England. He said he had a mate who was involved in football and that they shared a mutual interest in racing pigeons. Said his name was Gerry Francis.'

A trial was arranged, at the end of which Paul was offered a contract by Rovers. 'I went back and told Wilma there'd been a slight change of plans. The rest is history.'

Having signed for The Pirates in January 1989, Paul and his team mates just missed out on promotion, but the following season saw them finish champions of the old Third Division and get to Wembley in the final of the Leyland Daf Cup. 'Having come into the pro game at twenty-four, to be part of that golden era for Rovers was very special to me.'

But a well-publicized bust up with manager Francis nearly ruined everything for Paul. 'The week leading up to the Wembley game was full of tension for me personally. I'd had a big falling out with Gerry and that hadn't done my chances of playing on the famous pitch any good at all.'

Paul clinched his place in the squad though, after scoring in Rovers' last league game, away to Blackpool. A second half sub in the final against Tranmere, Paul still feels hard done by that they lost by the odd goal in three. 'We were so unlucky.'

But, after 43 games and six goals for Rovers, Paul took up an offer to play in Hong Kong. 'I went there on loan and was then offered a two-year contract. I was due back at Rovers, but Gerry realized what a great opportunity it was for me and I stayed with his blessing.'

During his time in Hong Kong, Paul picked up three championship medals and four cup winners medals, before returning to New Zealand with daughters Holly (born in Bristol) and Jessica, who was born in Hong Kong. Two further children, Matthew and Georgia, were born in 1997 and 1999 respectively.

After gaining the necessary qualifications, Paul took up a teaching post with Melville High School in Hamilton, where he is head of physical education.

Paul in his Rovers days.

Paul (second from left) enjoying a drink with friends in New Zealand.

MALCOLM NORMAN

Looking back, former Rovers goalkeeper Malcolm Norman realizes that he got his big break in professional football thanks to cricket. 'In the fifties, many footballers also played cricket and, as the end of the cricket season and the start of the football season overlapped, it could cause problems,' explained Malcolm. 'One of Rovers' keepers at the time was Ron Nicholls, who was also a very good cricketer with Gloucestershire. Rovers manager Bert Tann was not best pleased when Ron said he would not be playing soccer until after the cricket season was over, so he released Ron and told his scouts to find him another goalie – and quick.'

Rovers Welsh scout Wally McArthur had the answer to Tann's problems. He'd spotted Malcolm playing non-league football for Cardiff Corinthians and soon Malcolm was on his way for trials at Eastville.

'Rovers made me feel very welcome,' recalled Malcolm. 'They had me down to play in reserve games at West Ham and Watford and Bert Tann told me he was looking for a keeper that would dominate his area and catch crosses. I did just that and Mr Tann signed me on.' And Malcolm had an unexpected signing-on bonus – bed and breakfast. 'We were returning by train from the Watford game, which had been a night match, when I realized I was going to miss my connection for Cardiff. I ended up staying at Mr Tann's.'

Malcolm signed as a full-time pro in May 1958, but a fractured wrist bone suffered during pre-season training, put the blocks on his progress.' I was in a hospital bed when the season kicked off, having had the bone removed. Then, when I left, I had to get fit for selection.'

Malcolm made his belated first-team debut for Rovers against Leyton Orient at Eastville and kept his place for much of the season. Over the next four seasons, he was to make around 80 senior appearances. One game that stood out was a home fixture with Leeds United. 'They had a young Jack Charlton at centre forward and we went in at half time four-nil down and expecting a rollicking. But Bert Tann was brilliant – he gave the best team talk I ever heard and gave us back belief. I can still hear him saying "you can do this"– and we came back to draw four each.'

Other games that stood out for Malcolm were Rovers' first match under floodlights at Eastville, September '59 versus Ipswich, and a record breaking crowd of 38,472 (never beaten) for the cup tie at home to Preston in January 1960.

Eighteen months after joining Rovers, Malcolm was on stand-by for the Welsh national side. 'Arsenal's Jack Kelsey was the regular Welsh keeper, but was doubtful for a game against England. The Welsh FA contacted Rovers for my release but, unfortunately for me, Jack was fit enough to play.'

But, at the end of the 61/62 season, Malcolm left Rovers – one of the victims of the player clear-out following relegation from the (old) Second Division. He was to have two seasons with non league Kidderminster, before enjoying Western League success with Welton Rovers.

Away from soccer, Malcolm was a technical salesman and, following retirement, a volunteer driver for the Avon Ambulance Service.

Married to Joan, the couple live in Midsomer Norton. They have three sons and five grandchildren.

Malcolm and his team mates look on in despair, as Liverpool score in a Second Division game at Eastville.

Enjoying his garden, Malcolm Norman today.

MARK O'CONNOR

Winger Mark O'Connor arrived at Bristol Rovers in the saddest of circumstances in the summer of '84. Tribal rivalry across Bristol had been forgotten with the heartbreaking news that Eastville favourite Mike Barrett had cancer. Within weeks he died, aged just twenty-four. Mark was the player brought in to take his place on the left wing.

'David Williams signed me for Rovers after Mike had been diagnosed with the illness,' recalled Mark. 'I didn't know Mike personally, but it was obviously a very sad time for everyone associated with the club – very sad indeed.'

Born in Rochford, Essex, Mark began life as a professional footballer with Queens Park Rangers, playing there under two of soccer's most colourful characters. 'Tommy Docherty was the manager when I started off as an apprentice,' said Mark. 'Later, Terry Venables took over and he gave me my league debut against Chelsea when I was eighteen-and-a-half. He went on to get the side to the FA Cup Final, which we lost to Spurs.'

After a handful of games for QPR, Mark was loaned out to Exeter City, where Gerry Francis was in charge. 'I had eight months there and enjoyed it,' he said. 'It's never quite the same playing reserve-team football and when you make the step up it's a case of sink or swim. The move to Exeter really launched my career and I played about forty games for them.'

Mark's all-action displays down the flank for 'The Grecians' soon attracted the scouts and brought about his move to Rovers, albeit in such sad circumstances. 'Rovers had some good players at the club, particularly Geraint and David Williams, who controlled the midfield,' recalled Mark. 'I played left wing and Ollie (Ian Holloway) was on the other flank and, on our day, the side was a match for most teams in the (old) Third Division.'

During his two years with Rovers, Mark was to make over 80 senior appearances, scoring 11 goals. He also picked up two caps for the Republic of Ireland Under-21s. And, much to the delight of Rovers fans, he was never on the losing side when it came to local derbies with Bristol City. 'I played five times for Rovers against City and never lost one,' he said with a grin. 'I remember one FA Cup game at Ashton Gate. We were one down, but came back to win three-one and I got one of the goals. Given the local rivalry, that was a bit special.'

With David Williams gone and new manager Bobby Gould rebuilding, Mark decided it was time for a change and joined Bournemouth. It was to prove the start of an ongoing working relationship with team mate (and also former Rover) Tony Pulis.

'I had two or three seasons at Bournemouth and then three years at Gillingham,' continued Mark. But a broken leg spelt the beginning of the end for Mark's playing days. and, under 'Gills' boss Pulis, he joined the club's coaching staff.

Having obtained the necessary coaching badges at Lilleshall, Mark progressed through the ranks, staying part of Tony's coaching team as he went on his management stops at Stoke, Portsmouth, Plymouth, an ill-fated stay with Bristol City and, finally, Stoke again, where Mark is first-team coach.

Mark and wife Clare live in Dorset with son Sam and daughter Lucy.

Mark in league action for Exeter City.

A key member of Stoke City's coaching staff, Mark O'Connor today.

LINDSAY PARSONS

If you're ever chatting with Lindsay Parsons, don't mention 'the one that got away'. Not that the former Rovers full back has got anything against war films or fishing, it's just that, after a league career of nearly 500 games, the goals scored column, which reads 'none' should actually read 'one'.

'It was in 1971, an FA Cup tie against Cambridge United at Eastville,' recalled Lindsay. 'I hit a twenty-yard drive which found the back of the net, but team mate Bruce Bannister said he got the last touch and claimed it.'

Born in Bristol in 1946, Lindsay was playing local youth football when he was spotted by Rovers. Joining The Pirates as an apprentice when he left school was a natural progression, as was his signing full-time on his eighteenth birthday. 'I made my debut a month after signing pro, a four-nil home win over Notts County,' he said.

Lindsay was to enjoy 14 seasons with Rovers, clocking up 409 appearances, including 167 consecutive games. 'There were some very good players and some brilliant characters during my time with Rovers,' said Lindsay. And the best of them all? 'Alfie [Biggs] – without doubt,' was his instant reply.

Having spent so long in the Rovers line-up, Lindsay has a host of fond memories. 'Winning the Watney Cup in '73, promotion from the old Third Division the following year and becoming club captain in 1976 are just a few of my special memories of Bristol Rovers.'

But, in 1977, a parting of the ways, as Lindsay left Rovers to finish his playing days at Torquay United, where he went on to make another 56 appearances over two seasons.

'After football I worked for Rolls Royce for a while and managed Frome Town and Cheltenham Town, who were non-league then,' he said.

But then came the chance to get back into league football and forge a partnership with a former team mate, which is still thriving to this day. Ex-Rover Tony Pulis took over as manager of Gillingham and asked Lindsay to be his number two. 'We got promotion in our first season there and then took the club to the First Division Play Off Final the following year,' said Lindsay proudly.

After four years at Gillingham, the duo moved on for an ill-fated six months' spell managing old rivals Bristol City.

'That was a massive disappointment,' admitted Lindsay. 'We knew we were up against it at Ashton, but we got so much stick it was unbelievable. We even got a couple of death threats!'

After City, the pair had nine months at Portsmouth, helping the club avoid relegation. A boardroom take-over saw them leave 'Pompey' and it was to be two years before they resumed their partnership, this time at Stoke City, again managing a successful fight against the drop in their first season.

In September 2005 they moved on to Plymouth Argyle, before Pulis was enticed back to Stoke. Lindsay stayed on at Home Park, as another former team mate, Ian Holloway, took over the reins. But Pulis without Parsons is like fish without chips and it was odds on that the pair would be reunited. And so it proved to be, with Lindsay now back with Tony at Stoke, where he is chief scout.

Married to Wendy, the couple still live in the family home in Bristol and have three children, Amber, Hollie and Billy.

Bristol Rovers player Lindsay Parsons.

Off on a scouting mission, Stoke City chief scout Lindsay.

MARTIN PAUL

'It's every lad's dream to become a professional footballer, but you have to go into the game with your eyes open to the fact that it might not work out, disappointing though that is,' said Martin Paul philosophically, reflecting on his short career with Bristol Rovers.

Born in Lancashire in 1975, Martin moved down to the West Country in 1979. His footballing skills as a youngster won him county recognition and by 1992 he was playing in Rovers youth team, finishing up as the side's top scorer. His progress continued in the reserve side after he'd signed professional forms and when he was called up to the first team, it seemed the world was his oyster.

'John Ward was Rovers' manager at that time and he gave me a two-year-contract and the chance to play in the first team,' said Martin. 'He was an excellent man-manager and very fair and straight with his players.'

But, after a handful of senior starts, Rovers let him go. 'I had verbally agreed a new contract with the manager for another year, but before anything was put in writing, John got the sack and that was that,' revealed Martin. 'Also, as a striker, goals are your life blood. I got one in my eleven starts for Rovers, but I hit the woodwork four times. Who knows what would have happened if they had gone in.' The one that did go in came in a 2-0 home win over Brentford in September '95.

Martin's bad luck continued when he made the move to Doncaster Rovers. 'I had a two-year contract there, but, unbeknown to me when I signed, the club was in severe financial difficulties and it was a near-miracle if we actually got paid. The PFA were called in, but weren't a great deal of help and, as nobody can live on fresh air, I left.'

A brief spell in Belgium followed, before Martin returned home to sign for Bath City. Here he came into his own and between November '96 and July 2001 he netted 96 goals for 'The Romans'. A £3,000 transfer fee took him to Newport County, where he spent a season. The next stop was Chippenham Town, before Martin returned to Twerton Park to score more goals for Bath. His final tally for the club came to 104 goals in 200 senior games, making him the team's most prolific scorer since the days of Paul Randall.

Mangotsfield United was Martin's next port of call, before he returned to Twerton Park yet again, answering an SOS by his old club as they hit an injury and goalscoring crisis. Away from soccer Martin is a recruitment consultant for a company specialising in the construction industry. He lives in Emersons Green with his partner Leigh and has a young son, Harvey, from his previous marriage.

'When I look back, I don't have any regrets at all,' summed up Martin. 'You could wonder what could have happened if you'd done things differently, or if circumstances were different, but life's a bit too short for all that and I'm just glad I had the chance to give it a go.'

Martin in his Bristol Rovers days.

Time for table-top football with young son Harvey.

SHAUN PENNY

'In for a penny, in for a pound' – that's how the old saying goes. But, in the case of Bristol Rovers, it was more 'in for a Penny in for £20,000'. For that was the fee that they were reported to have paid neighbours Bristol City for striker Shaun Penny back in 1979.

'When I left City, I was going to go to Crystal Palace, but Terry Cooper, who was coaching at Eastville at the time, persuaded me to stay in Bristol and join Rovers,' said Shaun.

An England schoolboy international, Shaun joined The Robins at the age of 15, on the understanding that, with professional football being such a precarious business, his education came first. 'Mum wanted me to complete my schooling, so City agreed to send me to Millfield for two years, which wasn't too bad as they had excellent sporting facilities,' revealed Shaun.

After his two years at the South West's highly rated public school, Shaun joined the City groundstaff, before signing on as a full-time professional. But, despite finding the net regularly for the reserves in the Football Combination, he didn't make the break through into the first team. Why? 'I really don't know – you'd have to ask Alan Dicks!' was his reply.

After switching to Rovers, Shaun settled in quickly and a goal against Preston early on at his new club, plus a brace against Chelsea, won over the Rovers fans.

'There was a great atmosphere at the old Rovers' ground [Eastville] and we would regularly get big crowds,' recalled Shaun. 'Do you know, Ollie [Ian Holloway] was an apprentice at the time and used to do my boots.'

So which players stood out during his time with Rovers? 'David Williams was very good, as was Gary Mabbutt – very professional.'

During his three years at Rovers, Shaun was to play for Bobby Campbell, Harold Jarman, Terry Cooper and Bobby Gould. He made 60 league appearances, scoring 13 goals for the side, before he left for pastures new. 'The club was in financial difficulties and there was a lot of cost cutting going on. I left by mutual consent.'

After Rovers, Shaun tried his luck playing in Finland for KTP Kotkan, based near Helsinki. 'It is a beautiful country and the football was about Third Division (now League One) standard. And the language wasn't a problem – they speak English better than we do! The only trouble was that I went over the day after my son was born and, although we were going to move over there, it never happened. Also, I was the only Brit in the side, which didn't help me settle, so I came back after a year.'

On returning to the UK, Shaun played in the local non-league circuit for Weymouth, Dorchester, Forest Green, Gloucester City, Clevedon Town and Bath City (twice). It was during his second spell at Bath that Shaun stepped up to assistant manager, a role which he went on to carry out at Backwell, Mangotsfield and Clevedon Town.

For the past 16 years or so, Shaun has run his own property development business. 'I started at the bottom in the building trade and worked my way up,' he pointed out. Shaun lives in the Filton Park area of Bristol with long-term partner Lucy. The couple have a young daughter, while Shaun has a son and daughter from his previous marriage.

Shaun in his Bristol Rovers days.

Now in property development, former Rovers striker Shaun Penny.

NICK PLATNAUER

The profession of postman has proved to be the most popular for City and Rovers players leaving the game. Former Pirate Nick Platnauer is just one of a number of former Bristol players who have swopped deadball deliveries for first-class deliveries, as he rattles the letter boxes of Leicester.

Nick began his footballing days playing for his local side, Bedford Town. 'Trevor Gould was the manager and his brother Bobby was assistant manager at Chelsea,' said Nick. 'I was combining playing football with working as a cashier at a bank, when Bobby moved on to manage Bristol Rovers and agreed a fee with his brother to take me to Bristol.'

Nick soon adapted to life as a full-time pro. 'It was all new to me, but I was only young (21) so it held no real fears and I knew that full-time training and playing with quality players would only improve my game,' he pointed out.

Nick singled out Paul Randall, the Williamses (David and Geraint), Phil Bater, Keith Curle and Ollie (Ian Holloway) as some of the players that made an impression on him.

'Then they brought in Alan Ball,' exclaimed Nick. 'What a fantastic education and honour to be in the same side as the great Alan Ball. I played alongside him in his last three games for Rovers and it's something I won't forget in a hurry.'

After 24 games, seven goals and just over a year at Rovers, Nick moved up a couple of divisions, when he linked up again with Gould, who had left Rovers to manage Coventry City. Rovers received £50,000 for his transfer and Nick went on to play around 60 games for the Highfield Road club. 'It was a big step up for me, with fantastic facilities and the opportunity to play against the big teams.'

In December '84, Nick switched to Midlands rivals Birmingham City. 'We got promotion in my first season there, but overall it was a disappointing time and I didn't play particularly well,' he admitted. A three-month loan spell at Reading was equally disappointing, with Nick restricted to just a handful of games as the harsh winter saw many matches postponed.

'After that I had three-and-a half seasons at Cardiff,' went on Nick. 'Frank Burrows signed me and, although I've played for quite a few managers, he was the best.' During his time at Ninian Park, Nick picked up the Player of the Year award on three occasions.

Two years at Notts County followed, where Nick was part of the team that won promotion in two successive seasons. 'Neil Warnock was manager – now he was different!' laughed Nick. 'Mind, he could always generate a good team spirit.'

In January '91 Nick had a 14-game loan spell at Port Vale, before joining Leicester City. Moves to Scunthorpe, Mansfield and Lincoln followed in the next three years, before Nick moved on to the role of player-coach with non-league Bedworth. He went on to hold a similar position at Blue Square North side Hinckley United, before taking up the manager's role at Rothwell Town.

After three years at Rothwell, Nick returned to his roots by becoming manager at Bedford Town, guiding the club to promotion to the Conference South. He stepped down in January 2007 and is now assistant manager back at Hinckley United.

Married to Tina, the couple have two sons and a daughter.

Nick in his Bristol Rovers days.

Nick Platnauer today.

FRANKIE PRINCE

Over the years, every football team included what was commonly known as 'a ball winner'. They still do. A 'fear nothing, give it and take it' type of individual, whose job is to go in where it hurts to gain his side possession of the ball and, often as not, let the opposition know he is there. Such a description more than adequately fits Frankie Prince and, after over 400 games in Rovers colours, there are sure to be plenty of former opponents who would testify to Frankie's ability in that role. In fact, a few of them are probably still carrying the scars!

These days Frankie is looking to pass on the benefit of his experience and often under-stated skills to the soccer stars of tomorrow, all part of his role as a Football in the Community Officer at Torquay United.

'After I finished playing, I worked as a nursing assistant in a Dawlish Hospital for eighteen months,' said Frankie. 'Then this job came up. I've got all the necessary coaching badges and really enjoy my work – taking football into the community.'

A veteran of over 400 games for Rovers, Penarth-born Frankie was a product of the club's excellent South Wales scouting network. After working his way through the youth and reserve sides, Frankie was signed on as a full-time professional, making his debut in the old Third Division against Swindon.

A first team regular long before his twenty-first birthday, Frankie's all-action displays soon made him an Eastville favourite. Not that his tough tackling style pleased everyone.

Many an opponent walked away limping after clashing with the player that manager Don Megson described as his 'Sherman tank'. And the pencil industry probably did a roaring trade, as referees frequently found themselves reaching for their notebooks – and they weren't asking for an autograph!

'Derby matches against City were always very special,' he recalled. 'I used to have some right tussles with Gerry Gow, who was very similar to myself in the way we played – but he was also a very good footballer.'

Looking back, Frankie fondly remembers the 1972/73 Watney Cup success and promotion the following year. 'I had to come off late in the second half with a broken toe in the Watney Cup Final and watched the rest of the game from the touchline. We won on penalties and keeper Dick Sheppard was the hero, with a vital penalty save in the shoot out. His early death was a tragedy.'

Altogether Frankie pulled on Rovers' first-team shirt 419 times, scoring 26 goals. In addition, he won four Welsh Under-23 caps. 'I also made the full squad for a game against England and although I didn't get on, it was a fantastic experience.'

In 1980 though, Frankie and Rovers went their separate ways. 'It was a wrench leaving the club after so long, but I wasn't seeing eye to eye with the manager, so it was time to go.'

Frankie moved on to Exeter City, playing over 30 games for 'The Grecians', before stepping down from League football and finishing his playing days in local non-league.

And, as Frankie goes about his job, taking football to the community and perhaps coaching a star or two of the future, you wonder how many potential Football League ball winners will emerge from their time under Frankie.

Frankie in his Rovers days.

Football in the Community Officer Frankie Prince today.
(photo: *The Sunday Independent*)

TOM RAMASUT

There used to be an old BT advert based around the theme 'it's good to talk'. One person who would agree wholeheartedly with that sentiment is former Bristol Rovers midfield player Tom Ramasut. Mind, he does have a vested interest – he has his own mobile telephone business. 'I run a company called Xtramobiles, based in Cardiff,' said the former Welsh Under-21 international.

Born in the Welsh capital, Tom was on Rovers' books as a schoolboy, but took up an offer to join Norwich City. 'I was with Norwich from the age of fourteen and signed for them as a full-time pro at eighteen,' he revealed. Released by manager Gary Megson after a year as a professional, Tom weighed up his options, before deciding to try his luck a second time with Rovers.

'Going back to Bristol was ideal – it was a lot nearer home for a start,' continued Tom, who made his league debut for Rovers in an away match at Bury. 'There was a great team spirit at the club and everyone bonded well on and off the pitch.

'My first season was spent avoiding relegation, but the second year we were pushing for promotion and got knocked out in the Play Off semis by Northampton, after taking a three-one lead in the home leg. It was a real body blow and some of the lads were in tears.

'Looking back, there were some very good players at Rovers,' pointed out Tom. 'Jamie Cureton, who was also the club joker; Andy Tillson, one of the best and most complete professionals and captains I've played with and, of course, Ollie. He hated losing, even when it was just a knock about in training.'

But after two seasons and around half a century of games for Rovers, a contract dispute saw Tom walk away from the club. 'I was young and a bit naïve,' admitted Tom. 'My agent convinced me that I was worth more than the club was offering and told me to hold out for better terms. In the end I think Ollie lost patience and I left, but, with hindsight, I think I should have taken their offer and stayed.'

After Rovers, Tom had a two-month trial with his home-town club Cardiff, but was carrying a groin injury that subsequently required an operation and left. He did the rounds on the South Wales soccer circuit at Llanelli, Barry Town, Haverfordwest, Merthyr and Carmarthen Town. It was while he was with Barry Town that Tom first experienced European football. 'We played full time at Barry and won the double – the league and the Welsh Cup – two years running and subsequently played in the Champions League as a result. I also played in the UEFA Cup for Carmarthen, after winning the Welsh Cup for a third time.

'After that I moved up to London and worked for an estate agent, while playing semi-pro for Aylesbury in the Ryman League, before dropping out of football for a while,' he revealed. Tom later returned to Wales and rejoined Carmarthen Town, before signing for another of his former Welsh clubs, Haverfordwest.

'Looking back, I would have loved to have stayed with Rovers and, if I could turn the clock back, I wouldn't have left,' he summed up.

Former Rovers man Tom Ramasut.

Now running his own mobile telephone company, Tom Ramasut today.

JOHN RUDGE

All too often fan pressure can get football managers the sack. A few bad results and some disappointing performances and the supporters are howling for blood. So it's refreshing to find someone so revered by the fans that the opposite happened – they demonstrated BECAUSE the manager was sacked. That's what happened in the case of former Rovers striker John Rudge.

At the end of his playing days, John took over the manager's chair at Port Vale. During 19 years at the club he won promotion three times, took the team to Wembley on three occasions, generated over £10million in transfer income and made national headlines with some stirring FA Cup runs.

'The supporters were fantastic to me,' said John. 'But, after nineteen years the Board felt it was time for me to go and I was sacked.' Vale fans certainly didn't share the Board's views, though. They had a march through the town centre wearing flat caps – John is rarely seen without his flat cap during the colder weather – and organized a supporters' celebratory dinner for him, with 750 of them in attendance. 'I'll never forget that, as long as I live,' he said.

Born in Wolverhampton, John was spotted playing junior football by Huddersfield Town. He signed for 'The Terriers' as a 15-year-old, going on to make his debut against Swansea in the old Second Division in the 61/62 season.

In 1966, with just a handful of senior games under his belt, John moved on to Carlisle United. 'They had an excellent all-rounder called Chris Balderstone, who was a good friend and the club was managed by Alan Ashman, an excellent manager.'

After three years and over 50 league appearances for the Cumbrian side, John moved to the other end of the country, signing for Torquay United. 'They had a decent side in those days,' said John, who enjoyed three years there, playing over 100 games and scoring around 40 goals.

Over at Bristol Rovers, manager Bill Dodgin was keen on bringing John to Eastville, while his own striker, former Torquay legend Robin Stubbs, fancied a return to his old club. A move that suited all parties saw John head for Bristol and Stubbs back to Devon.

'I enjoyed my time with Rovers,' said John. 'We lived in Downend and settled in well.' John was to spend the best part of three years with 'The Gas' and fondly remembers winning promotion and the Watney Cup during his time there. 'There were also the two cup games against the mighty Manchester United, when we drew at home and won the replay at Old Trafford.' John scored in both those games.

In March 1975, after nearly 100 games and 22 goals, John left Rovers for Bournemouth. 'The move was a bit of a disappointment, as I had Achilles tendon problems that restricted me to just a couple of dozen games,' he revealed.

A spell as number two under former Rovers team mate Mike Green at Torquay followed, before John moved up to The Potteries, where, after a spell as assistant manager, he etched his name in Port Vale folk lore as manager.

After Port Vale, John became director of football for Vale's bitter rivals, Stoke City. 'It can be a tricky job and changes every time there's been a new manager, but I enjoy it,' said John.

Married to Dellice, the couple live in The Potteries. They have two daughters and three grandchildren.

John during his days at Rovers.

A typical picture of John and his flat cap.

ROBBIE RYAN

'Ronaldo? He's so fast and tricky, I couldn't even catch him to swap shirts at the end of the game!' So said Robbie Ryan, who had the thankless task of trying to mark the Portuguese star in the 2004 Cup Final, just before joining Rovers.

Born in Dublin in May '77, Robbie represented Ireland at youth and schoolboy level, going on to win a dozen Under-21 caps. 'I was spotted by a Huddersfield Town scout and went for a trial with them at sixteen,' said Robbie. After impressing the powers that be at Huddersfield, Robbie returned home to finish his education, before heading back to the Yorkshire club to start a career in soccer.

'My first manager was Neil Warnock and he was very good to me, letting me have time off to go back to Ireland and visit the folks,' said Robbie. Neil Warnock, never a manager to stay in one place long, moved on and was replaced by Brian Horton. When he left, new manager Peter Jackson brought in several new players and it was time for Robbie to think about his future.

With just 15 senior-league games behind him, Robbie moved to Millwall in January '98. 'I had the best part of seven seasons there and loved it.' During his time at The New Den, Robbie experienced the disappointment of just missing promotion via the Play Offs, promotion the following year to the First Division (now the Championship) and a near miss to the top flight, when Millwall came second best to Birmingham City in another Play Off nail biter. And, of course, his last season – 2003/4 – culminated in that Cup Final appearance marking the mercurial Ronaldo.

With his contract up, Robbie was offered a 12-month deal by the club. 'I wanted a two year contract. Also, I'd heard that the club was signing a new left back. As it turned out they didn't, but by that time Rovers had come in for me.'

Joining Rovers in the summer of 2004, Robbie was looking forward to the new challenge. 'Rovers are a big club that had been underachieving and had a good set up.' But it didn't start particularly well for the full back. 'The manager [Ian Atkins] wanted to play with wing backs, whereas I'd been used to playing in a flat back four,' he pointed out. 'It caused a few problems and I wondered why the devil he'd signed me in the first place.'

Robbie was to play 40 league games in his first season and admits to enjoying his football again after Atkins left to be replaced by Lennie Lawrence and Paul Trollope. But his second season with The Pirates was an injury-plagued one. 'I had ankle problems, knee problems - it was one injury after another. By the time I was fit, the side was pretty settled and the club agreed to release me in order to get first-team football.'

That was in January 2006, but the injury hoodoo stayed with Robbie as he sought contracts with Northampton Town, Brentford and Dagenham & Redbridge. 'I had trials with all of them, but kept breaking down.'

Former Millwall team mate Stuart Nethercott, the assistant manager at Welling United in the Blue Square South League signed Robbie up, while regular employment came via a job with a cable maintenance company on the London Underground. 'It's a good craic, with a good bunch of lads and I enjoy it.'

Former Rover Robbie Ryan.

Robbie Ryan today.

DAVE SAVAGE

Irishman Dave Savage started his football career in Kilkenny. 'I played for Kilkenny City when I was seventeen,' said Dave. 'It was about the standard of the (old) English Fourth Division and a very good learning curve for a young lad.'

Dave's footballing skills in Kilkenny's colours soon alerted the football scouts from 'over the water' and he joined Brighton & Hove Albion. 'I had a two-week trial and got an eighteen month contract,' he revealed. But Dave's first venture into English football was interrupted by injury and he had eight months out of the game, following a bone fusion operation.

'It was while I was recovering that the club got relegated and also experienced severe financial problems, so I returned to Ireland, determined to get fit.'

Dave was to spend a year-and-a-half with Longford Town in the League of Ireland, before leaving Irish shores again, this time bound for Millwall. 'Millwall were in the old First Division when I joined them and I had five seasons there,' said Dave, who went to play over 200 games for the club and win five Under-21 and five senior caps for his national side.

In 1998 Dave moved on to Northampton, managed by Ian Atkins. 'I didn't know a lot about the club when I signed for them,' he admitted. 'They came across as ambitious, had a brand new stadium and, in Ian Atkins, had a manager who could sometimes seem strange, but knew so much about the game.'

Three years and over 120 league games later, Dave joined Oxford United. 'It was actually Mark Wright who signed me – Ian took over as manager later,' explained Dave, who played over 100 games for them, during which time he won the coveted Player of the Year award.

It was in the summer of 2003 that Dave moved to Rovers, where he would ultimately link up for a third time with Ian Atkins. 'I enjoyed playing for Rovers. The supporters are so passionate about their football team and were tremendous, even when we struggled.'

It was Ray Graydon who signed Dave, Phil Bater taking over the reins as caretaker manager, following Graydon's departure in 2004. 'It was unfortunate the way it worked out for Ray Graydon, especially going back to manage a club where he'd done so well as a player,' said Dave. 'Phil Bater, a good chap, again with a great Rovers past, took over in difficult circumstances, before Ian [Atkins] came in. He brought in some quality players, but just couldn't turn the club's fortunes around.'

Dave was to clock up 65 league appearances in Rovers' colours. 'I had a real feeling for Rovers and was proud to wear the shirt,' said Dave.

In the summer of 2005, a chance to play back in the Northamptonshire area was too good to refuse and Dave signed for Rushden & Diamonds. 'Rushden were still in the Football League then and I had two seasons with them. I even played for them against Rovers at The Mem and got a good reception from the home fans.'

After his spell with Rushden, Dave dropped down to non-league soccer, playing for Brackley Town and later, Oxford City in the Southern Premier. 'I still play for them part time, working as a brickie during the week.'

Married to Jackie, the couple have two young children, Megan and Eireann and live in Northampton.

Dave in action for Northampton.
(photo: Pete Norton Photography of Northampton)

A drop of the Irish black stuff for Dublin-born Dave.

JOHN SCALES

As a young footballer, John Scales couldn't, in his wildest dreams, have imagined how his career would take off, when he was released by his first club, Leeds United. But the faith and judgement shown by Rovers' manager Bobby Gould set him back on the road to soccer success, with multi-million pound moves to three of the country's top-flight clubs, FA Cup and League Cup winners medals and three caps for England.

'I joined Leeds as an apprentice in 1984, but after fifteen months they told me I wasn't going to be offered a professional contract.'

The decision to release John, along with other promising youngsters, was more to do with the club's ailing finances than footballing ability and John was thinking of leaving the pro game to become an architect. 'Then I got a call from Bobby Gould at Rovers offering me a trial – and the rest, as they say, is history.'

Equally at home as a full back or centre half, John soon made his mark at Rovers, playing nearly 100 games for The Pirates between 1985 and 1987. 'When I first joined, David Mehew, who was an old team mate at Leeds, also came in, so there was one familiar face for me, which was good. I was a long way from home, but the players and the fans at Rovers were great and I really enjoyed my time there,' he said.

His wholehearted approach and steady defending soon caught the eye of the bigger clubs, but it was the man who had saved John's career, Bobby Gould, who stepped in to give him his big chance in the top flight. 'Bobby had moved on to Wimbledon and they paid Rovers £75,000 to take me there.'

John was to enjoy seven seasons with Wimbledon, coming on as a substitute in their historic FA Cup Final win over Liverpool, winning the club's Player of the Year award in 1989 and going on to make nearly 300 appearances.

In September '94, Liverpool paid out £3.5 million to bring John to Anfield. He went on to win a League Cup winners' medal the following year, plus the first of his three England caps. 'It was a fantastic move for me, one of those clubs that most footballers can only dream of playing for,' he admitted.

John went on to make over 100 appearances for the mighty Liverpool, but in the winter of 1996, Spurs splashed out nearly £3million to move him to White Hart Lane. But John was plagued by injuries. 'It was a massive disappointment to me. I had muscle injuries, calf strains, hamstring problems. I saw umpteen specialists, had operations and all the time I was stuck on the sidelines.'

With just a handful of appearances for Spurs, John was released and attempted to kick start his career at Ipswich Town. 'I was desperate to get back playing again, but it was an uphill battle and, after a handful of games, I knew it was over. It was almost a relief in the end.'

Since then, John has been heavily involved in the business of sport, first setting up an international sports licensing and merchandising agency and building up his European sports events company, Be Sport. He has been a major player in the kit4schools initiative and is involved in TV and media production.

Living in Wimbledon village, John is married to Lisa, and the couple have a young daughter, Mabel Rose.

John in action for Bristol Rovers.

John today.

JUSTIN SKINNER

Piece of trivia for you. The first Rovers player to score a goal on his debut as a substitute was Justin Skinner. Rovers record signing from Fulham in August '91, he grabbed his new team's consolation goal, in a 2-1 defeat to Newcastle United at Twerton Park.

'I'd been at Fulham for six years and this was my first move, so it was a bit daunting for me, but good to get a goal under my belt so early in my Rovers career,' said Justin.

During his time at Craven Cottage, Justin had made well over 150 senior appearances for the London side, before Rovers manager Martin Dobson paid out £130,000 to bring him to Twerton. 'I never really got to know Martin all that well, as he was replaced not long after I signed,' pointed out Justin. 'After that I played for three or four managers there. John Ward was a very good organizer and Ollie (Ian Holloway) was – still is – very passionate about the game. Then there was Malcolm Allison. Very much a larger than life type of character, I don't think he really rated me. Even so, I learnt a lot about man-management from him. In fact, I'm sure I learnt a lot from all the managers I played for, even from the mistakes they made.'

Between his arrival in 1991 to his departure in 1998, Justin was to make around 200 appearances for Rovers, scoring 11 goals. He was a member of the side that lost in the Division Two Play Off Final against Huddersfield in 1995. 'It was a boyhood dream to be able to play at Wembley,' said Justin. 'But to lose what was such an important game for everyone at the club left a bit of a sour taste.'

In March '98, Rovers let Justin out on loan to Walsall. 'Just as had happened at Rovers, the manager got sacked shortly after I joined,' said Justin. 'I thought to myself, here we go again!'

With his career seemingly on a downward trend, things suddenly perked up for the midfielder. 'Out of the blue I got a call from Alex McLeish, asking me if I fancied signing for him at Hibs – I jumped at the chance,' he said. And so Justin moved north to spend six years in Scotland, first with Hibs, then Dunfermline and finally Brechin, playing over 100 games in the Scottish League.

'I loved it in Scotland – one of the best times I've had in football. We made some fantastic friends up there and still go back to visit.'

After Scotland, Justin returned to London and spent two years or so at Chelsea, coaching the youngsters as part of the club's academy and youth development programme. He moved on to Loftus Road and for a time was the club's reserve team manager, before becoming assistant manager at non-league Lewes, helping the club win the Conference South championship in 2008, before a parting of the ways.

Not so long ago he made a nostalgic return to Twerton Park. 'It was strange to be back at the place which had been part of football life for so long,' he said. 'Great memories.'

Married to Jane, the couple live in Berkshire and have two sons – Harry and Jack.

Justin in his Rovers days.

A more recent photograph of Justin, taken on a return visit to Twerton Park.

GARY SMART

'If I had a pound for every person who's asked me about that goal, I'd be a very rich man by now,' said former Bristol Rovers midfield player Gary Smart.

'That goal' – back on New Year's Day 1987 – was very important to Rovers fans, a late match winner against arch-rivals Bristol City at Ashton Gate. 'The ball just sat up nicely and I caught it perfectly,' recalled Gary. 'Scoring the only goal of the game against City in front of nearly twenty thousand spectators – real Roy of the Rovers stuff.'

Born in the blue half of Bristol, Gary grew up near Eastville. Taken to his first game at the age of four, his dreams of playing for his team were shattered when, after playing junior football for The Pirates, he was turned down for an apprenticeship.

'I got a job as a maintenance engineer and was playing local amateur football when I got the call, asking me if I'd like to turn out for Rovers reserves as a non-contract player,' said Gary. 'I played in one particular reserve game, at Brighton, and it was rumoured that the then Brighton manager, Alan Mullery, was interested in signing me. That spurred Rovers into giving me a professional contract.'

But even though he'd made the step up to fully-fledged professional footballer, Gary declined to go full-time. 'I simply couldn't afford to give up the 'day job' and go full time at Rovers,' confessed Gary. 'I was earning more as a maintenance engineer than I would do as a full-time Rovers player.'

Between 1985 and 1987, Gary was to make just over 20 senior appearances and score (including the one at Ashton Gate) four goals.

'Playing part-time presents its own problems,' admitted Gary. 'Fitness was never an issue, but it was the time you take in training to rehearse set pieces and so on that I was missing out on. Bobby [Gould] was nagging me to go full time and said he'd do something about getting me a decent contract. Then he left for Wimbledon!'

With Rovers a club in turmoil on and off the pitch, Gary cut his ties, walked away from the club and signed for Cheltenham Town, a non-league side in those days. After Cheltenham, Gary joined Wokingham, before making his mark at Bath City, playing over 300 games for 'The Romans'. Spells at Mangotsfield, Forest Green, Newport County and Gloucester City followed, before he took up assistant-manager roles with first Clevedon Town and later Bath City.

'When Alan Pridham was sacked as manager at Bath, I had one game as caretaker manager and the Board offered me the job until the end of the season, but I wouldn't take it. Alan was my best mate and it wouldn't have been right.'

An electrical mechanical engineer, Gary is married to Emma and they live in the Downend area of Bristol with their two children, Joshua and Cloe.

Gary in his footballing days.
(photo: *Bath Chronicle*)

Pictured at his place of work, Gary Smart today.

ROBIN STUBBS

'The best signing I ever made.' That was the verdict of Bill Dodgin, when he brought prolific goalscorer Robin Stubbs to Eastville in the summer of 1969. And Rovers gain was Torquay United's loss, with Robin's legion of fans not believing that the club had let their star player go and, to make it worse, for a paltry £12,000.

'I enjoyed my time with Rovers, they played good attacking football, which suited me right down to the ground.'

Born in Smethwick, Robin first made a name for himself with Birmingham City. 'West Brom was my nearest club and I did train with them as a youngster,' he pointed out. But it was rivals Birmingham who signed Robin. An injury crisis saw him in the first team at 17 and he never looked back, as he went on to play over 80 games and score more than 30 goals for the club.

'Arthur Turner was my first manager at St Andrews and, although the team usually struggled for top flight survival, we did enjoy some success in European matches,' said Robin.

When Gil Merrick took over the manager's chair however, it was time to move on. 'I just didn't get on with him, so I asked to go on the transfer list,' said Robin. Although it meant dropping down three divisions, Robin, like a lot of former Birmingham players at the time, moved on to Torquay, who paid out a club record fee of £6,000. 'I fell in love with the area, still love it,' he said.

Over the next six seasons Robin became a cult figure for fans at the seaside club. Altogether, he finished top scorer for the club in five out of six seasons, including one season when he found the net 39 times. But then manager Allan Brown decided to rebuild the side and sold Robin to Rovers.

'Rovers were a very strong team in that division and were always around the top six, without quite gaining promotion,' said Robin. And the team mates he remembered at Eastville? 'There were a lot of good players,' he mussed. 'Frankie Prince, Harold [Jarman], Bobby Jones and the goalkeeper, Dick Sheppard. He was a good friend long after we finished playing – his death at such an early age was tragic.'

In his second season with The Pirates, Robin entered the record books as the first Rovers player to score four goals in an away (league) game – a 4-1 victory at Gillingham – and for the second successive season he was the club's top scorer. But his Rovers career was cut short. 'I picked up a bad knee injury, but would play on with it strapped up, which ultimately meant an early retirement from the game,' said Robin. He was also taken ill with glandular fever during his time in Bristol, but could still look back on a highly creditable return of 32 goals from 93 league appearances during his time with the club.

When the chance came to return to Torquay, it was too good for Robin to turn down, but, sadly, injury meant he was never to relive the glory days again at Plainmoor.

After leaving the game, Robin worked in the printing business, before taking on a local sports initiative with Torbay Council, giving sports coaching to physically handicapped and able-bodied children.

Married to Joanne, the couple have two teenage sons – Christopher and Ben.

Robin of the Rovers.

Robin Stubbs today, relaxing at his Torquay home.
(photo: Stuart MacDowell)

JOHN TAYLOR

Bristol Rovers have had some pretty useful centre forwards over the years and John Taylor could certainly be counted as one of their most successful. In his two-and-a-bit seasons at the club, he made around 100 appearances, scored 45 goals and, by the end of his career, had over 500 games to his credit and over 150 goals.

John's early dreams of making it as a footballer were dashed when his local club, Colchester United, released him in 1983, without a single first team game to his credit – a decision they've no doubt regretted ever since. His first spell at Cambridge – he later returned to play and manage them in the later stages of his career – saw him net 46 goals, many coming in an explosive goal-scoring partnership with Dion Dublin.

Then, in March 1992, a transfer saw Taylor swap places with Rovers' favourite Devon White, with Cambridge also paying out £100,000 as part of the deal. 'I managed to find the net early on in my time with Rovers, which is always a big help when you want to win the fans over,' pointed out John. In fact, he scored 13 goals in his first 13 games, to make him a crowd favourite.

Practically an ever present over the following two seasons, John bagged 23 goals in 93/94 – the highest total since Alan Warboys some 20 years earlier. 'I really enjoyed my time at Twerton Park,' said John. 'I was living near Keynsham, got on really well with the fans, who were terrific, and thought the club had some excellent players.'

Sadly for Rovers fans, John left in the summer of '94, after a contractual dispute, Bradford City, managed by Lennie Lawrence, paying Rovers £300,000 for him.

John's spell at Valley Parade began well and he netted 11 league goals in 36 games, before Luton Town splashed out £200,000 to take him back to East Anglia. But the move never really worked out. 'I was carrying a back injury which didn't help,' pointed out John, whose return of just three league goals was nothing like his previously prolific scoring record.

Loan spells at Lincoln, managed by his former Cambridge boss John Beck, and original club Colchester followed, before Cambridge won the race for his signature to bring him 'home.' John was to enjoy seven more years with 'The Us,' adding another 40 goals to the previous 46 he'd bagged for the club. After hanging up his boots to take on the reserve team manager's position, he was given the job of first team boss in the winter of 1992.

'Looking back, the opportunity probably came too early in my career,' admitted John, who was forced to make a playing come-back, following the sale of star striker Dave Kitson. With the side struggling at the wrong end of the table, John's long association with the club ended in March 2004, when the Board decided on a change of management. Shortly afterwards, a spell at Northampton finished prematurely, after John's season was disrupted by thrombosis of the leg, which put him out of action for six months.

'After football I was an insurance agent and then I sold mobile phone tariffs,' said John, who returned to the non-league scene with Dagenham & Redbridge, Mildenhall Town and Long Melford. He went on to manage Newmarket Town in the Eastern Counties League, as well as coaching youngsters in the Cambridgeshire area.

John (left) challenges for the ball.

Coaching the young stars of tomorrow.

GARY WADDOCK

A former Republic of Ireland international with 22 full caps, Gary Waddock has made over 500 league appearances, played in the FA Cup Final (and replay) at Wembley and given sterling service to six league clubs, including two years and over 70 games for Rovers.

'I came to Rovers in November '92,' recalled Gary. 'Dennis Rofe signed me – and a week later he'd gone!'

Thirteen years before joining The Pirates, Gary had broken into the first team at Queens Park Rangers, a club that was to take up a large slice of his footballing life. 'I had come up through the youth system there and made my debut at seventeen,' he explained. That was in 1979 and over the next eight years he made well over 200 league appearances for the club, including two Wembley Cup Final appearances.

'We got to the final in '82, which, for a Second Division club, was a marvellous achievement,' he said. 'We drew the first game one-all after extra time and lost the replay one-nil. Two cup finals in a week – a bitter sweet experience, but something I'll never forget.'

But a ruptured medial ligament threatened to end Gary's playing days at an early age.

'The experts said I was finished, but I was determined to carry on playing and went to Belgium for two years and built up my fitness playing for Charleroi.'

Gary returned to London in 1989, signing for Millwall, where he made over 60 appearances, before 'going home' to QPR. The return to Loftus Road didn't work out though and he moved on loan to Swindon Town, before Rovers came in for him.

'Twerton Park was certainly different from some of the grounds I'd played on, like Wembley. But the fans, with their brilliant backing of the team, turned it into a real fortress and not many sides liked playing there.'

Gary remembers that after Dennis Rofe had left the club, the legendary Malcolm Allison took charge. 'Now there was a character,' laughed Gary. And someone else who left an impression on Gary during his time with Rovers, was striker Marcus Stewart. 'What a player. You could see he was destined to go all the way,' he said.

After Allison, John Ward brought much needed stability to the club and Gary went on to play over 70 games for the club, before finishing his playing days with a four-year spell at Luton Town.

Having decided to stay in the game after his playing days, Gary took his coaching badges, returning to QPR, who were then under the wing of Ian Holloway and coached the academy, the youth and reserve teams, before being appointed caretaker-manager in February 2006. The arrival of former team mate John Gregory as manager the following September saw Gary have a short spell as assistant manager, before a parting of the ways a month later.

But Gary was soon back in management, charged with the task of getting Aldershot back into league football – a challenge he rose to superbly, as Town swept all before them to win the Blue Square Premier championship and promotion back into the Football League.

Married to Marie, the couple live near Aldershot with their young daughter Channel.

'I've had lots of highs and lows in my career and my only regret is that I'm not seventeen and could do it all over again,' summed up Gary.

Gary Waddock the Rovers player.

Addressing the supporters at an Aldershot fans' forum.

ALAN WARBOYS

Back towards the beginning of this look-back at former Pirates, there's an article on prolific Rovers goalscorer Bruce Bannister. Well, there was no way that this book could be completed without including the other half of that dynamic Rovers striking duo of the seventies, Alan Warboys.

Alan arrived at Eastville some 15 months after fellow Yorkshireman Bruce. 'We hit it off straightaway, on and off the pitch, and have remained firm friends ever since,' said Alan.

A typical old-fashioned centre forward, Alan began his career with Doncaster Rovers, coming up through the junior ranks. He made over 50 league appearances and scored a dozen or so goals for 'Donny', before a transfer to (old) First Division side Sheffield Wednesday in the summer of '68. Seventy-one league appearances, 13 goals and 18 months later, he moved on to Cardiff City and, in his two-and-a-half seasons at Ninian Park, maintained a healthy average of a goal practically every two games.

A disappointing 18 months at Sheffield United followed that, before Alan made the move to Eastville, Don Megson paying out a club record £35,000 for his services. 'I signed for Rovers towards the end of the '72/73 season – the start of four fabulous years in Bristol,' he recalled.

With the Warboys-Bannister goal machine firing on all cylinders, the lethal combination carried on where they left off in the 73/74 season and helped steer Rovers to promotion from the Third Division, Alan netting 22 of their league goals in that year. And four of them came in one historic game. 'Ah yes, Brighton away…' mused Alan, as he thought back to that day when Rovers hammered a Brian Clough-managed Brighton 8-2 at The Goldstone Ground in front of the national media, with Alan getting four of the goals. 'I was in the treatment room after the game, having a cut in my head attended to, when Cloughie stormed past. He stopped alongside me and said; "That must have been self-inflicted young man, my defenders didn't get anywhere near you all afternoon!"

'The thing with Rovers was that we all gelled together on and off the pitch, it was a real family club.'

Alan lived at Stapleton during his time at Bristol and he went on to notch 60 goals in his 164 games for The Pirates. But, after four years, and with the 'Smash and Grab' partnership broken up when Bruce moved on to Plymouth, Alan departed, signing for Fulham.

A year after his move to Fulham, Alan was reunited with Bannister when he signed for Hull, but they were never able to repeat the highs of that partnership in their Rovers heyday.

Alan's career went full cycle when he signed for his first club, Doncaster Rovers, finishing his career there three seasons later in 1982.

'After football I ran a pub for eight years, then I packed that in and for the past sixteen years I've been driving for a local haulage firm,' said Alan.

Married to Carol, the couple have one son, Alan junior, who is director of sport at a school in Doncaster. They also have two grandchildren.

'I've lots of great memories of my time with Rovers and have kept my scrapbooks and even got a couple of videos from my time there,' said Alan. 'I have been back once, to see them play at The Mem, but it's not the same as Eastville and football has changed so much, it's not the game it was.'

Alan (right) with strike partner Bruce Bannister.

Alan Warboys today.

BRIAN WILLIAMS

With so many games these days being won or lost in the lottery of a penalty shoot-out, it must be reassuring when you've got a spot kick specialist or two in your side. One man that could certainly qualify as a 'spot kick king' is Brian Williams.

'It's all a question of confidence,' said Brian, most of whose goals during his 17 years in the Football League came from the penalty spot. 'I used to vary my spot kicks, but the other thing, apart from confidence, is, once you've decided where you're going to put the ball, never change your mind.'

Born in Salford, Brian began his career with Bury. After becoming 'The Shakers' youngest-ever debutant at the age of 16 years and 133 days, he went on to notch up nearly 200 games for the club over six seasons. In 1977 a £70,000 transfer fee saw him move to Queens Park Rangers in the old First Division.

'There were some very good players and characters there,' recalled Brian. 'Don Masson, Johnny Hollins, Dave Webb and Stan Bowles. One of my best memories was being in the side that beat the mighty Liverpool 2-nil at Loftus Road.'

After around 50 appearances for QPR, Brian moved on to Swindon Town. 'Bob Smith, who had been my manager at Bury, was in charge of Swindon at the time, so he knew me pretty well and must have rated me to sign me,' pointed out Brian.

Brian was to enjoy three seasons at The County Ground, playing in the side that lost out in the semi-finals of the League Cup to Wolves. 'It was over two legs and we took a 2-1 lead to Molineux, before being beaten in extra time – one of my biggest disappointments in football,' he revealed. The side also made the last eight of the FA Cup, before being knocked out by Spurs. 'I was marking Glenn Hoddle that day and we were winning one-nil with ten minutes to go, before they scored twice to go through. That was another disappointment.'

A contractual dispute saw Brian pack his bags, with Terry Cooper bringing him to Rovers. 'I learnt so much from Terry,' said Brian, who had four years at the club. 'At one stage, the midfield there consisted of Williams, Williams and Williams, with David and Geraint playing alongside myself.

'The fans were very good to me at Rovers,' added Brian, who notched up over 200 games for The Pirates, many of them as captain. 'It's always an honour to captain a side and I've been captain at all my clubs, with the exception of QPR.'

A move across town saw Brian link up once again with Terry Cooper, then managing arch rivals Bristol City. During his two seasons at Ashton, Brian added over 90 more appearances to his CV, including leading the side out for the Freight Rover Trophy Final at Wembley.

After City, Brian had two years with Shrewsbury Town, before winding down his playing days with non league Alvechurch. He went on to become a coach/football in the community officer for Hereford United, before his old club, Shrewsbury, invited him to take up a similar position with them.

Married to Andrea, the couple live in the Shrewsbury area. They have a son, Oliver, who was on Aston Villa's books until an accident put paid to a career in football, and daughter Chloe.

Rovers' penalty ace Brian Williams.

Brian Williams today.

DAVID WILLIAMS

'Looking back, Rovers led the way in youth academies, long before the two words became part of football vocabulary.' So says former Pirate David Williams, who went on to play over 400 games for the club that he captained and managed.

Born in Cardiff, David's natural ability as a schoolboy was noted by Rovers' well established South Wales talent spotters. 'At sixteen I was offered professional terms by Rovers, but my parents wanted me to continue my education, so I stayed on to take my A Levels and then went on to teacher training college,' revealed David. It says much for the talented midfielder's determination that he went on to gain all his necessary qualifications while coming through the ranks from A team to reserves to first team.

In fact, for three seasons David was a first-team regular while still at college and later while teaching. 'Bobby Campbell persuaded me to go full time in 1978 and I decided that the time was right to put teaching on hold.'

A firm fans' favourite, David's next career move came completely out of the blue. 'Manager Bobby Gould had left the club to take over at Coventry,' recalled David. 'It was the last game of the season, I was injured and the Board asked me to help take charge of the team. Not long after, I was offered the job of player-manager.'

And so began a two-year period with the Welshman in charge. But, in 1985, David decided that he needed a new challenge. 'I'd made up my mind that it was time for something new and, as I didn't want anyone to think I was being underhand, I announced my decision before the last game of the season.'

David was a little concerned as to how the fans would take the news. He needn't have worried. 'At the final whistle the supporters ran on the pitch and carried me off shoulder high. It was quite emotional.'

A £40,000 transfer fee took him to Norwich City, where his all-action displays brought him to the attention of the Welsh selectors and he went on to win five caps for his country. Having played 60 senior games for Norwich, he had five years as assistant manager and even a short spell as caretaker manager of the national team, before spending 18 months as assistant manager at Bournemouth. After that, he had coaching roles at Everton, Leeds and then Man United.

'The lure of Manchester United was too good to turn down. I had five fantastic years there and during my time we brought through some great youngsters.'

Strangely, despite David's success at Old Trafford, Fergie decided to change the staff around and David found himself out of a job. 'The problem is, where do you go after Manchester United?'

Used to getting pupils through exams, David became a driving instructor. 'I did that for nine months,' he revealed. 'It kept me busy and was just a different form of teaching from what I'd been used to.'

In 2004 David made a welcome return to soccer, retracing his steps to Carrow Road to take on the role of youth coach, a post he held until retiring in 2007.

David lives in Harrogate with wife Mandy. They have a grown-up son and daughter.

David in league action.

David Williams today.
(photos: Norwich Football Club)

GERAINT WILLIAMS

Back in the eighties, three of the first names on Rovers team sheet was Williams. There was Brian at left back, attacking midfielder David and defensive midfielder Geraint Williams. These days Geraint has more than midfield-action to concentrate on, having taken on the manager's job at Leyton Orient.

'I learnt a lot from the managers I played under and also during my time as manager at Colchester and I hope I can carry that through here at Orient,' said Geraint.

Born in Glamorgan in 1962, Geraint joined Rovers as an apprentice, having, like many others, graduated through the club's Welsh nursery. 'Bobby Campbell was Rovers' boss at the time – a real character,' said Geraint. 'Do you know, just above the tunnel at Eastville was a sign 'Campbell's Kingdom' – shades of Bill Shankly's 'Welcome to Anfield!'

Terry Cooper gave Geraint his big chance in a first team that included the likes of Gary Mabbutt, David Williams and the late Micky Barrett. 'Terry believed in the youngsters, while coach Harold Jarman was a legend who made football fun,' said Geraint.

Already under the scrutiny of the Welsh selectors, having won Under-21 caps while at Rovers, an all action display at Derby County prompted Derby manager Arthur Cox to put in a £40,000 offer for the Welshman. 'We were moving into a new house,' said Geraint. 'We laid the new carpet on the Monday and the following day I was on my way to Derby. We never did get to move in!'

And so, after 169 games and 10 goals for The Pirates, Geraint switched to The Baseball Ground. With Geraint in the Derby midfield engine room, the club won promotion from the (old) Third Division, went on to win the Second Division Championship and, having established themselves in the top flight, finished a creditable fifth. 'That season we would have qualified for Europe, but it was during the time of the English ban, following The Heysel Stadium disaster,' pointed out Geraint. 'We had a very good side, which included Peter Shilton, Mark Wright and Dean Saunders. And Arthur Cox was an excellent manager,' he added.

After over 300 games and nine goals for 'The Rams', Geraint, who had established himself in the full Welsh national side, was packing his bags and off to Anglia, to sign for Ipswich Town. Here he enjoyed five seasons, making 200+ appearances, scoring three times.

In 1998 Geraint moved on to Colchester United. But after just 39 games for the Layer Road outfit, a bad knee injury spelt the end of his playing days. 'While I was trying to recover, the manager asked if I fancied looking after the reserve side and I found myself enjoying it,' he said.

After seven seasons as assistant manager, the club turned to Geraint to take control. 'Getting promotion to The Championship was a tremendous achievement for the club,' he pointed out. But a string of bad results in the 2008/9 season spelt the end of Geraint's first managerial appointment. Undeterred, he bounced back, accepting the task of repeating the success he achieved at Colchester with Leyton Orient.

Married to Lynne, the couple have a teenage son (Rhys) and daughter (Bethan) and live in Ipswich.

Geraint, in action for Rovers.

Geraint, no stranger to the media spotlight.
(photo: Colchester United Football Club)

JOHNNY WILLIAMS

For a man who was a driving force as an attacking wing-half (that's midfield these days) who gave sterling service to Plymouth Argyle and then Bristol Rovers, it was no surprise that the words 'driving' and 'service' were to continue to be so apt for Johnny Williams. For, after leaving professional football, he went into the garage business. 'At one time I had three service stations,' said Johnny.

Although he was to spend the bulk of his playing days with Argyle – he made over 500 appearances for 'The Pilgrims' – Johnny was actually born in Daventry Road, Bristol. 'We moved to Plymouth when I was quite young,' revealed Johnny, whose father had been a journalist with the now long gone *Bristol Evening World* newspaper.

An apprentice in the Plymouth Dockyard, Johnny was spotted playing in the local leagues, including for the docks team, by Argyle and was initially signed on amateur forms. 'I broke into the first team quite early and will always be grateful to manager Jack Rowley for giving me my big chance,' said Johnny.

Between 1955 and 1966, Johnny was to make over 500 appearances in Argyle's colours, including 179 consecutive games between December '58 and March 1963. He continued to play for Plymouth while doing National Service, during which he also played in an army representative side that included Bobby Charlton.

Surprisingly, Argyle accepted an offer of £6,500 from Rovers in December '66 and Johnny was on his way to Eastville. 'I looked on it as a new challenge – and, after all, I was born in Bristol,' he pointed out.

'Bert Tann was the Rovers manager in those days and I have to say I always got on very well with him.'

Johnny made his Rovers debut on 27 December against Orient and went on to make 68 league appearances for The Pirates. A wing half who always had an eye for goal, he scored 10 goals for Rovers, to add to the 48 league goals he netted for Argyle.

Part of the deal when he joined Rovers was that he was allowed to continue living and training in Plymouth. But when Tann moved 'upstairs' as general manager and Fred Ford took over the role of team manager, there was a problem. 'I never really got on with Fred Ford,' admitted Johnny. 'I don't think he liked me living in Plymouth, but that was agreed when I originally joined Rovers.'

And so, at the end of the 68/69 season, Johnny was released by Rovers. 'I went back to Argyle to help coach the reserves and the youth players,' he said. 'But when manager Billy Bingham left, so did I.'

Johnny enjoyed four or five seasons playing for local amateur side Falmouth Town. 'There were a lot of former Argyle players in the side and we won just about everything going,' he said.

Now in his seventies, Johnny still keeps his hand in at his remaining service station at Southway. 'My son John runs the business, but I still look in once a week,' he said.

Johnny and his wife Shirley recently celebrated their fiftieth wedding anniversary. The couple live in the Plymstock area of Plymouth and, in addition to son John, have a daughter, Debbie, and five grandchildren.

Johnny Williams in his heyday.

Now a very fit seventy-three, Johnny Williams today.
(photo: Tony Carney)

Another great book for Rovers fans from Redcliffe Press

Bristol Rovers Greats
Ivan Ponting and Richard Jones

Bristol Rovers may never have played in the top flight of the game but, down the decades, few clubs have had more colourful characters. In this book, the authors – both life-long followers of Bristol soccer – profile the most memorable of the post-war Pirates.

They are all here, from the vintage Eastville favourites of the 1940s and 1950s, through the Watney Cup heroes of the early 1970s, to the idols of Gerry Francis's blue-and-white army, and beyond: Geoff Bradford and Alfie 'The Baron' Biggs, Harold Jarman and Alan Warboys, Gary Penrice and Ian Holloway, Marcus Stewart and Nathan Ellington – the list is mouth-watering.

Bristol Rovers Greats is an affectionate and often revealing tribute to some of the most revered names in West Country sport.

£9.99

Available from bookshops or visit our website www.redcliffepress.co.uk